Cambridge Elements

Elements in Ancient and Pre-modern Economies
edited by
Kenneth G. Hirth
The Pennsylvania State University
Timothy Earle
Northwestern University
Emily J. Kate
University of Vienna

THE SHANG ECONOMY

Roderick Campbell
New York University

Shaftesbury Road, Cambridge CB2 8EA, United Kingdom

One Liberty Plaza, 20th Floor, New York, NY 10006, USA

477 Williamstown Road, Port Melbourne, VIC 3207, Australia

314–321, 3rd Floor, Plot 3, Splendor Forum, Jasola District Centre, New Delhi – 110025, India

103 Penang Road, #05–06/07, Visioncrest Commercial, Singapore 238467

Cambridge University Press is part of Cambridge University Press & Assessment, a department of the University of Cambridge.

We share the University's mission to contribute to society through the pursuit of education, learning and research at the highest international levels of excellence.

www.cambridge.org
Information on this title: www.cambridge.org/9781009565172

DOI: 10.1017/9781009285230

© Roderick Campbell 2025

This publication is in copyright. Subject to statutory exception and to the provisions of relevant collective licensing agreements, no reproduction of any part may take place without the written permission of Cambridge University Press & Assessment.

When citing this work, please include a reference to the DOI 10.1017/9781009285230

First published 2025

A catalogue record for this publication is available from the British Library

ISBN 978-1-009-56517-2 Hardback
ISBN 978-1-009-28522-3 Paperback
ISSN 2754-2955 (online)
ISSN 2754-2947 (print)

Cambridge University Press & Assessment has no responsibility for the persistence or accuracy of URLs for external or third-party internet websites referred to in this publication and does not guarantee that any content on such websites is, or will remain, accurate or appropriate.

The Shang Economy

Elements in Ancient and Pre-modern Economies

DOI: 10.1017/9781009285230
First published online: March 2025

Roderick Campbell
New York University

Author for correspondence: Roderick Campbell, rbc2@nyu.edu

Abstract: This Element constitutes a systematic attempt to preliminarily reconstruct the Shang economy based on contemporary archaeological and textual evidence. At the same time, the rapid pace of Chinese archaeological discovery and the increasing deployment of archaeological science means that there is a wealth of new information making a new synthesis both challenging and necessary. This synthesis was written from the perspective that the study of ancient economy necessarily proceeds from the construction of models and the systematic exploration of principal economic components, including their articulation and change over time. Setting the Shang in a comparative context with other ancient economies in this series, those principal components are the domestic and institutional economy, specialization, forms of exchange, and diachronic developments. It is hoped that with this organization, comparison with other ancient economies can be more easily made and the significance of the Shang case more clearly seen.

Keywords: archaeology, Shang, economy, political economy, craft production

© Roderick Campbell 2025

ISBNs: 9781009565172 (HB), 9781009285223 (PB), 9781009285230 (OC)
ISSNs: 2754-2955 (online), 2754-2947 (print)

Contents

1 Introduction 1

2 Domestic Economy 13

3 Institutional Economy 20

4 Specialization 30

5 Forms of Distribution and Commercialization 40

6 Economic Change Over Time 50

7 Future Directions 58

References 63

1 Introduction

This Element constitutes a first English-language systematic attempt to reconstruct the Shang economy based on contemporary archaeological and textual evidence. Article length treatments have dealt with aspects of Chinese Bronze Age economies (eg. Underhill and Fang 2004; Liu, Chen, and Li 2007; Campbell 2021b) and there are monographs that have touched on the topic (Liu and Chen 2003; Campbell 2018; Li 2019), but so far there has been no monograph length attempt to bring together the current evidence in English. Although Chinese language works such as *Shangdai jingji yu keji* (*Shang Dynasty Economy and Technology*) (Yang and Ma 2010) provide encyclopedic coverage of mostly textual evidence, their assumptions derive from older Marxist and traditional historiographic paradigms. Moreover, textual sources are scanty for the period and difficult to interpret making archaeological evidence the primary means to reconstruct the Shang economy. At the same time, the topic of the economy (as opposed to the Marxist stage of economic development) has only recently emerged as a focus of archaeological study within Chinese archaeology, the mainstream of which is still culture-historical and traditional historiographic in orientation (Falkenhausen 1993; Liu and Chen 2012a). Despite this, the rapid pace of Chinese archaeological discovery and the increasing deployment of archaeological science means that there is a wealth of new information making a new synthesis both challenging and necessary. I would argue that in order to understand an ancient economy, it is necessary to construct models, systematically explore principle economic components, and search for evidence concerning their articulation and change over time. The components selected for this series are the domestic and institutional economy, specialization, forms of exchange, and diachronic developments. By organizing the study in this way, the commonalities and particularities of the Shang case and Bronze Age Chinese economic developments in general can be highlighted and their significance more clearly seen in comparison with other ancient economies.

1.1 The Shang

The "Shang" of this Element title has multiple, overlapping referents. It is the second dynasty of China's indigenous historiographic tradition, supposedly ruling for twenty-nine generations from the founding king Tang, "the accomplished," to Di Xin whose regime was overthrown by a Western alliance led by the Zhou king Wu. Archaeologically, the Shang is both a period (ca. 1600 BCE–1050 BCE) and a material cultural horizon that covered much of North China (see Table 1, Figure 1). Finally, "Shang" is the self-referential

Table 1 North China archaeological periodization

Period	Sub-period	Associated Traditional Chinese Historiographic Period	Dates
Late Longshan		Sage Kings/Early Xia dynasty	ca. 2500–1900 BCE
Erlitou		Late Xia dynasty	ca. 1850–1600 BCE
Shang	Early Shang (Erligang/ Zhengzhou)	Early Shang dynasty	ca. 1600–1400 BCE
	Middle Shang (Huanbei-Xiaoshuangqiao)	Middle Shang dynasty	ca. 1400–1250 BCE
	Late Shang (Anyang/Yinxu)	Late Shang dynasty	ca. 1250–1050 BCE
Zhou	Western Zhou	Western Zhou	ca. 1050–771 BCE
	Eastern Zhou	Springs and Autumns	770–476 BCE
		Warring States	476–221 BCE

term for the polity and people-centered at Anyang in the divinatory inscriptions recovered there. For the purposes of this study, the focus will be on the Shang kingdom at Yinxu during the Anyang (Yinxu) (Campbell 2014; Campbell 2018) or Late Shang period (Zhongguo 2003; Shelach-Lavi 2015). The reason for focusing on this time and place is its abundance of information, especially compared with any earlier period. Yinxu has been excavated nearly continuously since 1928, pausing only for the Second Sino-Japanese (1937–45) and Chinese civil wars (1945–49) (Li 1977). Yinxu is also the time of the earliest corpus of deciphered texts written in the Chinese script – the oracle-bone inscriptions.

1.2 Sources

1.2.1 Later Texts

Texts putatively containing information concerning the Shang dynasty date from the early Western Zhou to the Han and range from inscriptions on ritual bronzes and dynastic hymns to universal histories. The most comprehensive of the later sources,

The Shang Economy 3

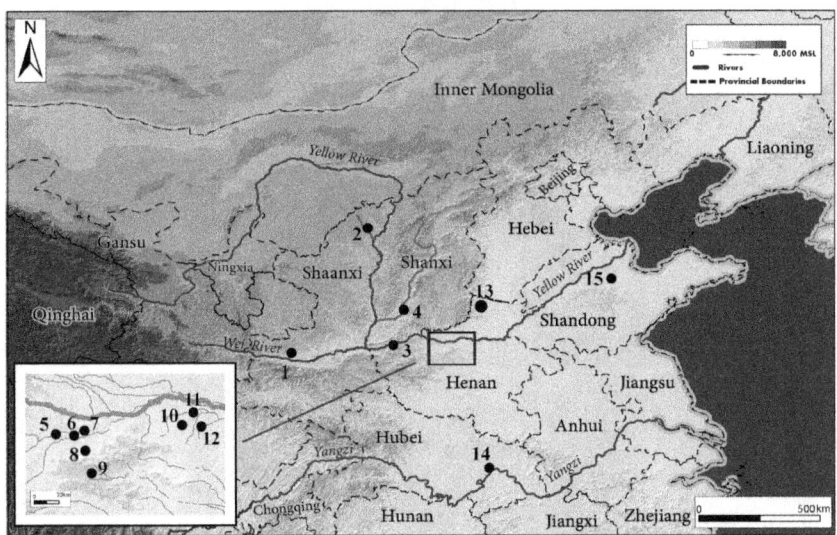

Figure 1 Location of major sites mentioned in the text. 1. Zhouyuan; 2. Shimao; 3. Guo; 4. Taosi; 5. Chengzhou; 6. Erlitou; 7. Yanshi Shangcheng; 8. Huizui; 9. Nanwa; 10. Guandimiao; 11. Xiaoshuangqiao; 12. Zhengzhou; 13. Anyang, Huanbei; 14. Panlongcheng; 15. Daxinzhuang
(redrawn from Campbell et al. 2022).

such as the *Shiji* (Records of the Grand Historian) or *Zhushu jinian* (Bamboo Annals), were written nearly a millennium after the fall of the Shang dynasty. Given that the histories are annalistic accounts of the doings of kings and other important persons, they tell us very little of use concerning ancient economy. More temporally proximate texts such as Western Zhou bronze inscriptions, the speeches of *Shangshu* (the Book of Documents), or the hymns of the *Shijing* (Book of Songs), are also of limited use in reconstructing the Shang economy, being at best fragmentary and indirect sources for reconstructing the economy and mostly reflecting the Zhou situation in any case.

1.2.2 Contemporaneous Texts

The first corpus of decipherable text in the Chinese script dates from the beginning of the Late Shang. These are mostly divinatory charges inscribed on bovine scapula and turtle plastrons (Figure 2). The topics, especially in the divinations of the oracle-bone inscription's first patron, king Wu Ding, range from weather to childbirth and from sacrifice to war. They are a remarkable window into the concerns of Shang kings, but they are also of limited value in understanding the Shang economy. The most basic reason is that as divinatory

Figure 2 Shang oracle-bone: inscribed turtle plastron
(Shijie yican Zhongguo 2008).

records they reflect uncertainty and so say nothing directly about routine matters. As royal divinations, they also mostly represent the things the king was concerned about personally as opposed to affairs delegated to others. For the Shang kings of the Late Shang, those concerns were mostly war, ritual, and the hunt. At the same time, silences can also be revealing, and the fact that royal divinations do touch on some economic matters but not others is useful in understanding some aspects of Shang political economy and the king's role in it. In addition to divinatory records, a small number of accounting inscriptions exist. The most common of these are notations on oracle-bones recording who contributed the bones and sometimes who prepared them. A second major inscriptional source is the Shang bronze inscriptions cast onto ritual bronze vessels. At the beginning of the Late Shang, these are mostly just names or "clan signs," but by the end, longer inscriptions appear with ancestral dedications as well as records of meritorious service and reward. Though these longer inscriptions are few in number and limited in scope, they provide lines of evidence complementary to those of the oracle-bone inscriptions.

1.2.3 Archaeology

Archaeological information exists in many forms and is the key means of reconstructing the Shang economy and its larger context. Shang archaeology has a history of nearly a hundred years and in this period there have been many changes in its goals and methods. This frequently means that early excavations were conducted in a way that makes their results difficult to compare with later work. In addition, for most of the twentieth century and with strong continuities today, Chinese archaeology was characterized by a major commitment to culture-historical approaches (Falkenhausen 1993; Liu and Chen 2012a). In the last few decades, this fundamental culture-historical approach has been complemented, nuanced, or even challenged by new methods and the rapid development of archaeological science within Chinese archaeology. On the one hand, this means that there is a huge and ever-growing quantity of archaeological research of diverse methodologies, and, on the other, that despite the rapid pace of work, many major sites still lack fundamental studies. This is especially true of archaeological research on economy, a topic that has only recently become a major focus.

All this is to say that our sources for reconstructing the Shang economy are full of holes and it is certain that any conclusions reached here will have to be revised as new archaeological information comes to light. Given this situation, the comparison of heuristic models and the synthetic analysis of as many lines of evidence as possible is critical. The larger diachronic context is also important for framing the Late Shang kingdom and understanding its place in the development of Early Chinese economies, while comparison with other ancient economies can be useful in developing models.

1.3 The Late Shang Kingdom in Diachronic Perspective (ca. 2500–1050 BCE)

1.3.1 Neolithic Foundations (ca. 2500–1850 BCE)

In the centuries before Yinxu, great centers rose and fell across the vast area of what is now the People's Republic of China. It has become increasingly clear in the last decade that the political and economic foundations of the Chinese Bronze Age were laid in the third millennium BCE (Yuan and Campbell 2009; Shelach and Jaffe 2014; Campbell et al. 2022). Large centers emerged along the Yangzi and Yellow river basins (Zhang et al. 2019). At the same time, wheat, barley, sheep, and cattle were introduced into Western China joining rice, foxtail and broomcorn millet, soybeans, pigs, and dogs to form regionally diverse but increasingly complex agricultural systems (Yuan et al. 2020; Lee et al. 2007; Li et al. 2014; Brunson et al. 2020). Craft production also saw rapid development in the third millennium, with evidence of jade working, production of fine ceramics, and the beginnings of metallurgy. Silk and lacquer artifacts were already being crafted in this period, and, if we can judge by later times, were probably of great economic significance. Unfortunately, however, neither preserve well in archaeological contexts and have not been systematically studied (Vainker 2004; Shelach-Lavi 2015).

K.C. Chang (Chang 1986) introduced the idea of "the Chinese interaction sphere" to describe the intensifying interactions of the Late Neolithic, or Longshan period (3000–1900 BCE). From an economic perspective, it is now clear that in addition to the prestige good exchange that has been in evidence since the 1980s, technologies such as bronze metallurgy, as well as new crops and domesticates also circulated. While the mechanisms for this exchange remain unclear, these technological introductions became components of increasingly complex and expansive economic systems. Large centers (ca. 200–400 ha) rose along with many of these regional economies. They were supported by a variety of increasingly broad agricultural economies (Yuan et al. 2020). The mechanisms for polity finance or urban provisioning are still unclear but preliminary evidence suggests regional diversity (Campbell et al. 2022).

1.3.2 The Erlitou Period (ca. 1850–1600 BCE)

There is debate about the chronology of the Erlitou site and its beginnings (Liu and Xu 2007; Campbell 2014; Jaang 2023) but it is uncontroversial to state that it had emerged as a regional center in Western Henan by 1750 BCE. Over the next century, it grew to a 300-ha site with many of the features that came to characterize the Central Plains Bronze Age (see Figure 3). For most Chinese archaeologists, Erlitou represents the last capital of the Xia dynasty. Whatever the historical affiliation of the Erlitou site, its explosive growth was accompanied by early material cultural heterogeneity, a pattern seen at later Central Plains centers. Erlitou sat at the center of the distribution of Erlitou culture sites that spread over much of Western Henan and southern Shanxi. While some have seen this in terms of a strongly centralized polity, others have argued against this interpretation (Liu and Chen 2003; Campbell 2014). Nevertheless, there is a mortuary hierarchy at the Erlitou site and large courtyard structures within a walled area that are generally interpreted as palace-temples.

The Erlitou site has evidence of bronze, turquoise, and bone artifact crafting near the palace-temple district (Zhongguo 2014) (Figure 3). Some scholars have interpreted this as "state" managed prestige goods production (Liu and Chen 2003), but the bone workshops at least are focused on producing a range of artifacts, and

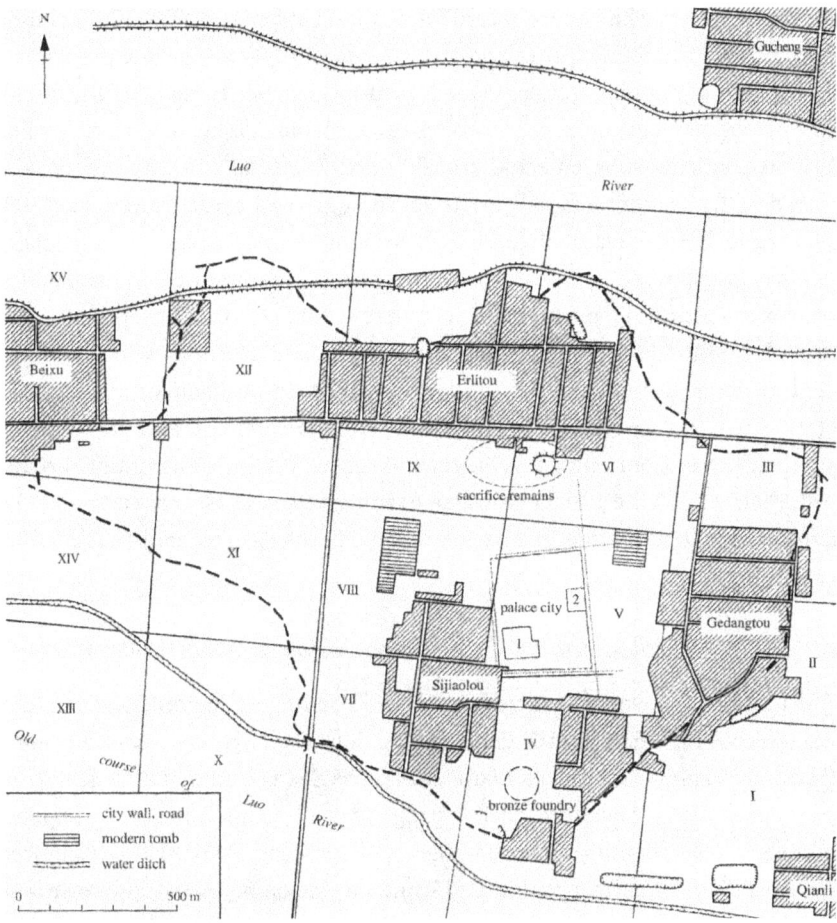

Figure 3 Erlitou site map (from Campbell 2014).

alternative models for them might be palace household provisioning or even commercialized exchange. Some prestige goods, such as white ceramics, were apparently produced in a number of places and widely distributed by elites beyond the capital (Liu, Chen, and Li 2007). Utilitarian goods like stone spades were produced in hinterland sites and exchanged in regional networks, apparently by non-elites (Liu, Chen, and Li 2007; Ford 2008). Taken together, the Erlitou polity craft economy includes large-scale, at least spatially centralized, prestige good production; decentralized prestige goods production and exchange; specialized small-scale production for a range of consumers; domestic production and the specialized production of utilitarian goods for local and regional exchange. These and other lines of evidence point to a complex crafting economy with much of it occurring outside of elite management.

The Erlitou site had an estimated population between 18,000–30,000 based on site size and estimates of population density of 60–100 people per hectare (Liu 2006) although other scholars argued for a lower estimate (Flad 2018). The paleobotanical and zooarchaeological work that has been done shows that Erlitou residents supplemented a basic millets, pig, and dog economy with rice, soy, fruits, and nuts as well as sheep, goat, and cattle (Lee et al. 2007; Zhongguo 2014; Yuan et al. 2020). These additional domesticates, especially grass-eating bovids, allowed for the expanded utilization of environmental resources. Mortality profiles and cart tracks suggest that sheep and cattle provided secondary products including wool and traction, while isotopic studies show that sheep and cattle had different husbandry practices (Li et al. 2014; Yuan et al. 2020). In terms of staple economy and urban provisioning, there is currently no evidence for grain storage or centralized redistribution, while elite rituals based on feasting sets suggest that status-related collective consumption events may have been a mechanism for food redistribution.

1.3.3 Zhengzhou and the Early Shang Period (ca. 1600–1400 BCE)

The Early Shang or Erligang period saw the rise of an unprecedented center at Zhengzhou (Figure 4). At 14–25 km in size, it marked a new watershed in early Chinese urbanism (Shelach and Jaffe 2014). The Shang center of Zhengzhou had an outer wall/levee and an inner rectangular wall estimated to have required between 365–110 million person-hours (Henansheng 2001: 1021; Campbell 2014: 123) for the outer wall and 55 million person-hours for the inner wall (Shelach and Jaffe 2014: 354). Most Chinese archaeologists associate Zhengzhou with an early capital of the Shang dynasty and see its rise, the establishment of the large walled site of Yanshi Shangcheng 6 km from the Erlitou site, and Erlitou's decline as marking the Shang conquest of the Xia (Zhongguo 2003). Early Shang culture spread over the previous distribution of Erlitou culture sites and beyond. This expansion is generally assumed to have taken the form of a conquest, and some scholars interpret Zhengzhou as the capital of a strongly centralized "state"(Bagley 1999; Liu and Chen 2003). Others, however, posit more heterarchical and dynamic models, pointing to examples like those of the Late Shang and the Western Zhou kingdoms (Campbell 2014, 2018). Like the Erlitou site, Zhengzhou was established as a regional center with a heterogeneous mix of material culture suggesting the diverse origins of its population (Henansheng 2001; Campbell 2014). Zhengzhou has evidence of hierarchy in both rammed earth courtyard structures interpreted as palace-temples and mortuary distinction. Although Zhengzhou Shangcheng is buried beneath the contemporary city of

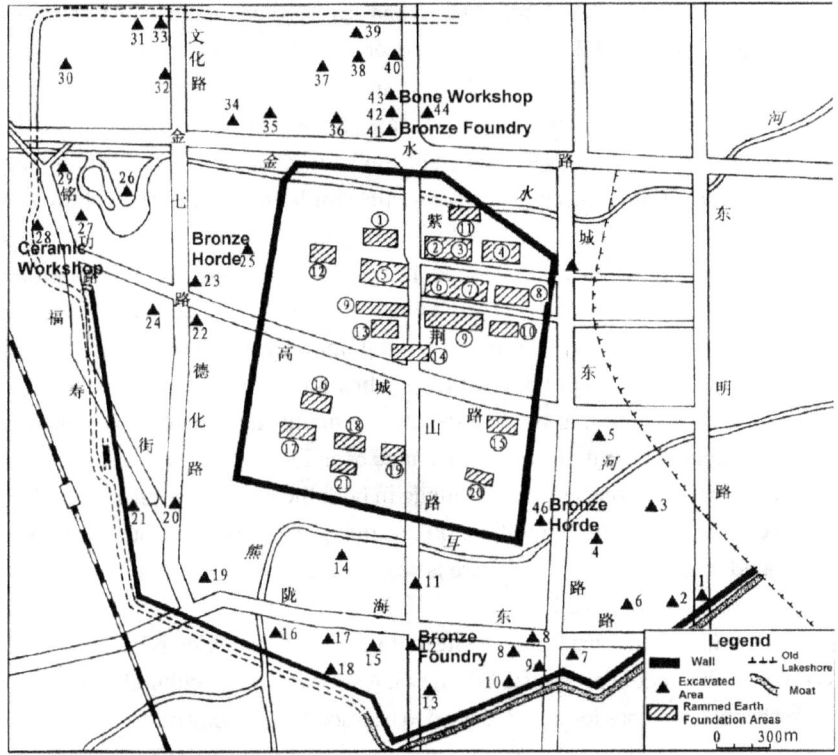

Figure 4 Zhengzhou site map (from Campbell 2014).

Zhengzhou and no royal or high elite tombs have been found, what tombs have been discovered nevertheless show greater evidence of mortuary stratification than those at Erlitou (Campbell 2018).

The production of ritual bronze vessels was greatly expanded at Zhengzhou both in terms of types and scale (Bagley 1999) and there were at least two major bronze foundries in simultaneous operation at Zhengzhou. There were also bone crafting and ceramic production sites at Zhengzhou although these were all excavated in the mid twentieth century and were never systematically studied (Henansheng 2001). On current evidence, all of the workshops appear to have produced products ranging from prestige goods to tools, weapons, and ornaments (Campbell et al. 2022), and though it is sometimes assumed that at least the prestige goods crafting was state-controlled (Liu and Chen 2003), there is no direct evidence to support this claim.

Depending on which population density and site size estimate is used (eg. Liu 2006; Campbell et al. 2022), Zhengzhou's population was between 40,000 and 130,000. A population of this size would have necessitated external provisioning. Although no granaries have been discovered at Zhengzhou, buildings that have been interpreted as storehouses granaries have been excavated at Yanshi Shangcheng (Chen 2021) and, more recently, what news reports call "state granaries" (Chen 2021). Nevertheless, what sort of staple economy this implies is unclear on current evidence, as is the scale and organization of the storage. No zooarchaeological work has been published for Zhengzhou, but preliminary work for Yanshi Shangcheng shows patterns similar to those at the Erlitou site. Archaeobotanical work at Zhengzhou suggests that increasing quantities of wheat were being grown in addition to millets, legumes, and rice. Wheat, millet, and legumes grown in rotation were key to later north Chinese multi-cropping regimes and it is possible that the increasing ubiquity of wheat signals agricultural intensification rather than just extensification.

Beyond Zhengzhou, scattered crafting remains have been excavated at Yanshi Shangcheng but no workshops have been located. These include bronze casting debris and bone crafting debitage in both the palace-temple area and the outer city. An area with multiple kilns and pottery production debris was excavated in the outer city and there is scattered evidence of stone tool production as well (Zhongguo 2013).

Another important Shang culture site of the Early Shang period is Panlongcheng. Located in the middle of Yangzi, but showing strong material cultural connections with Zhengzhou, it has long been argued to be a southern colony of the Early Shang kingdom set up to control local metallurgical resources (Bagley 1999; Liu and Chen 2003). Recent work has complicated the resource-extraction-outpost theory however, with evidence of local bronze casting and differences in the metallurgical sources of Panlongcheng and Zhengzhou bronzes (Liu et al. 2019). Additionally, Panlongcheng may have controlled the northward flow of prized middle Yangzi stoneware (Zhang 2014). These lines of evidence, along with the hundreds of kilometers between it and Zhengzhou, suggest that Panlongcheng may have been an at least partially independent polity rather than an extension of a centralized "state."

1.3.4 Middle Shang Period (ca. 1400–1250 BCE)

The Middle Shang or Xiaoshuangqiao-Huanbei period is named for the Xiaoshuangqiao site located near Zhengzhou and the Huanbei site located just across the Huan river from Yinxu. These are the major Central Plains sites currently known for the period. Later historical sources record a period of decline and division in the middle of the Shang dynasty. Xiaoshuangqiao is generally seen as a royal center during the decline of Zhengzhou, with large building foundations, sacrificial pits, tombs, and bronze casting remains (Zhongguo 2003; Campbell 2014). Huanbei, discovered in 1999, is a walled

150 ha site dating to the second half of the period and has seen more systematic work. A walled palace-temple area has been discovered in the center of the site, containing multiple large courtyard structures and sacrificial pits (Yinxu Work Team 2004; Jing et al. 2013). Bone crafting and bronze casting remains have also been discovered in a multi-crafting area and a preliminary study of bone crafting suggests extensive and highly skilled production, possibly for elite provisioning (He 2017).

1.3.5 Yinxu and the Late Shang Period (ca. 1250–1050 BCE)

Despite being the last capital of the Shang dynasty and, according to one reading of received historical sources, merely a partial restoration of its former glory, archaeologically, Yinxu or "the Great Settlement Shang" (as it was known in the oracle-bone inscriptions), is unprecedented. With new discoveries ever increasing its sprawl, the Great Settlement was over thirty-five square kilometers at its maximum extent with a population conservatively estimated at 100,000 (Figure 5). Yinxu was also a center of industry and ritual with at least four craft production areas as well as the central palace-temple district and the royal cemetery across the Huan river. Thousands of sacrificial pits mutely testify to the expanded scale of ritual at Yinxu while the royal tombs are on a scale never before seen in East Asia (Jing et al. 2013; Campbell 2014, 2018, 2022).

At the same time, and despite the dramatic concentration of people and resources in the center, evidence from the oracle-bone inscriptions – the first decipherable corpus of texts in ancient China – paints a picture of shifting alliances, frequent campaigns, and near-constant conflict within a decentralized political landscape. Indeed, the concentration of people in the center may have been a key aspect of the Shang polity – a political economy focused more on control of people than territory (Keightley 1983; Campbell 2018, 2021a). This ensured that the workshops of the capital crafted the finest things, that its rituals were unsurpassed anywhere and that the king could raise unmatched forces against his enemies. The concentration of population in a strong primate center is a feature of the Central Plains Bronze Age but seems to be taken to new heights at Yinxu. The association of certain crafts with elites and the concentration of industry within the primary center is also an old tradition but again is expanded and transformed at Yinxu with, it will be argued, profound ramifications for Chinese economic history. Finally, ritual, already a potential mechanism for redistributive feasting, takes on a new significance at Yinxu and with it the ritual economy in general. These developments all meant that Yinxu faced issues in provisioning beyond any earlier Chinese Bronze Age settlement. In sum, while Yinxu inherited a millennium of economic

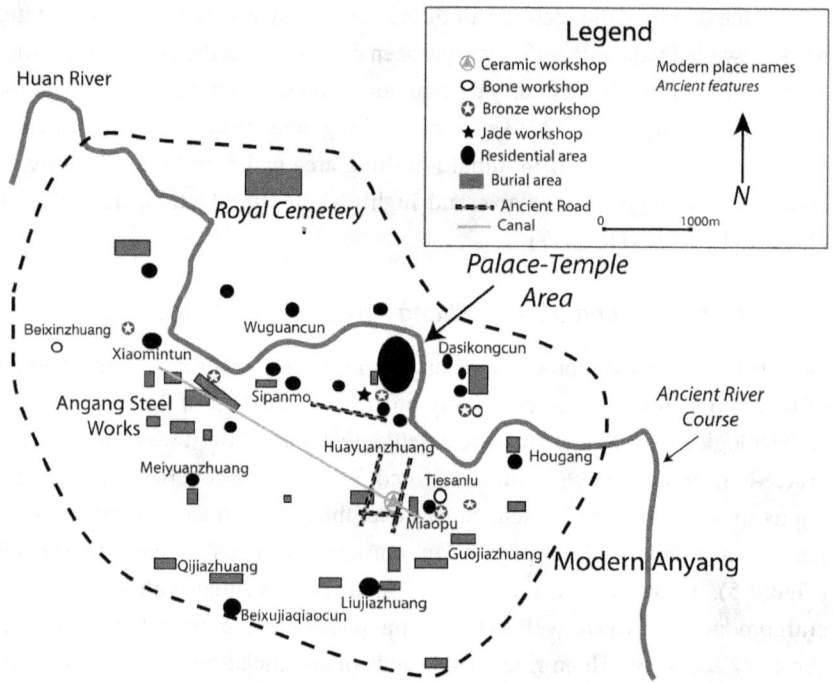

Figure 5 Anyang site map (redrawn from Campbell 2018).

development, it was also a period of transformation with important ramifications for later economic history.

In the following sections, I will present an argument for a new model of the Shang economy. This model proceeds from the assumption that royal power was both based on and limited by hierarchical lineages, indirect rule, and relatively inefficient transportation technology. Polity finance was based on mobility – mobile resources such as cattle and people were mobilized for labor or consumption but grain and other bulk goods were used locally. Taxes were in labor rather than kind and the king and his entourage traveled constantly, eating their way across the land. High-value resources or goods such as jades, horses, metal, cinnabar, and slaves were obtained though exchange mechanisms ranging from elite gifting to tribute and trade. The enormous capital was provisioned by the redistribution of sacrificial meat, urban farming, as well as nearby estates and, likely, markets. The numerous large-scale workshops of the capital were controlled by elite lineages and formed a basis of their economic power. These workshops produced goods for king and commoner alike and their development both drove and was driven by expanding commercialization. The ritual economy reached peak importance in the Late Shang period and contributed to nearly every aspect of economic life from food and clothing to burial. Rural sites were not self-sufficient but rather deeply integrated into local, regional, and inter-regional economic networks and commoners were involved in significant amounts of horizontal exchange. Finally, elite and non-elite commercial exchange was increasingly facilitated by the use of cowrie shells and perhaps other media.

2 Domestic Economy

The domestic economy is one of the most understudied aspects of Shang archaeology and history. Pertaining to the basic units of consumption, production, and exchange, the topic of domestic economy raises fundamental questions. What was the size of domestic units? What economic functions were performed at home, or by the household as a collective? What was the scale at which ownership and obligation operated? How did kin and class structures impact these things? Given the focus of scholarship on elites and prestige goods, none of these questions can be answered with any degree of accuracy. Nevertheless, by cobbling together various lines of indirect evidence and accidents of discovery, a partial picture of Shang domestic economy emerges.

2.1 Basic Economic Units

From a social, political, and possibly economic perspective, the fundamental unit of Shang society has long been understood to be the lineage (Chang 1980; Zhu 1990; Keightley 2000). Whether everyone was organized into lineages or only the elites has been a matter of debate (Campbell 2018), but the archaeology of the last two decades has moved the consensus toward the conclusion that lineages were fundamental to the organization of Shang society in general. The evidence includes the spatial organization of Yinxu (the Great Settlement Shang) as a collection of settlements with their own associated cemeteries and residential areas (Zhu 1990; Zhongguo 2003; Tang 2009; Jing et al. 2013; Campbell 2014, 2018). Settlement clusters include common wells and ritual deposits and houses often interspersed with tombs. Mortuary clusters combine elite and non-elite tombs, while the tombs themselves are structurally homologous across gradations of status, suggesting shared mortuary ritual and conceptions of the ancestors across the population. While the oracle-bone inscriptions and sacrificial deposits in the palace-temple area and royal cemetery demonstrate the importance of ancestors to the Shang kings, nonroyal divinations and bronze inscriptions dedicated to ancestors show that ancestor veneration was a central ritual focus for other elites as well. Non-inscribed oracle-bones are ubiquitous in Shang sites, even in remote villages like Guandimiao (Figure 1), as are ritual deposits, indicating that ancestral ritual and divination were not an elite monopoly (Hou et al. 2018; Li, Campbell, and Hou 2018). Given the importance of lineages for ritual and social organization, it is likely that some forms of property were owned at that level, as was the case in later China (Yates 2001: 291). Based on nonroyal oracle-bone inscriptions as well as the high degree of mortuary inequality, Zhu Fenghan (Zhu 1990: 172–73) has argued that elite lineage heads controlled the economic capital and wealth of the lineage, including land and herds.

2.2 Non-elite Domestic Economies

2.2.1 Urban Non-elites: Xiaomintun, Yinxu

From the perspective of non-elite residences, the basic unit of cohabitation cannot be much larger than a nuclear family. While few relatively intact non-elite residential areas have been published, the Xiaomintun locus at Yinxu (Figure 5) is an important exception. Excavated in 2003–2004, the Xiaomintun project was six hectares in area and discovered three clusters of non-elite Late Shang period houses dating to the first two phases of the site (Yinxu Xiaomintun Archaeological Team 2008). The residences were semisubterranean structures with one to five rooms with the most common being the one or two room type. They are somewhat atypical in that most dwellings at Yinxu were above-ground structures (Zhongguo 2003). The single-room houses ranged from 5 to 7 m^2, while the largest house was nearly 24 m^2. The clustering of the houses suggests separate residential groups. The houses themselves were structurally similar with the larger ones perhaps implying large family groups living together, a hypothesis strengthened by the multiple stoves and sleeping platforms in the multiroom houses. Given that the single-room houses are roughly the size of a US prison cell, it is difficult to image an extended family living there. The fact that the majority of the houses are of this small size suggests that the basic domestic unit for commoners was no larger than a nuclear family, even if multiple families lived together in residential groups. Though the most common size of residences across Yinxu excavations is estimated to be a little larger than this at 10 m^2 (Zhongguo 2003), this still implies individuals or single families were the basic units of domestic consumption. One implication is that most meals would have been prepared and eaten in small groups, a conclusion supported by work on Xiaomintun cooking pot sizes and animal bone breakage patterns (Zhang 2022). For urban dwellers, it is likely that there were garden plots between the settlement clusters and it is possible some also tended fields or herds beyond the Great Settlement Shang. Nevertheless, mortality profile analysis indicates a market meat consumption model and that most of the animals consumed at Xiaomintun (pigs, cattle, sheep, dogs, and a few deer) (Li 2009) were raised or hunted elsewhere. The uniformity and efficiency of butchery patterns, moreover, indicate the presence of skilled butchery specialists at Yinxu and that the residents of Xiaomintun did not generally butcher their own carcasses (Zhang 2022).

The people living in the Xiaomintun residential clusters were likely involved in the bronze casting industry located nearby and possibly buried in the adjacent cemetery. Indeed, most of the residences were abandoned during phase II and overlaid with later bronze-casting remains as the foundry grew in size in phases III and IV (Yinxu Xiaomintun Archaeological Team 2008). The association of residential groups with burial clusters has partially motivated the idea that Yinxu, the Great Settlement Shang, was composed of smaller lineage settlements clustered around the great royal lineage settlement with its palace-temples and royal cemetery (Chang 1980; Tang 2009; Jing et al. 2013). The hypothesis that each of these lineages had their own vocation is likewise widely held (Chang 1980; Zhu 1990; Cao 2018). In the case of Xiaomintun, since the full excavation report is still pending, there is no direct evidence available concerning domestic crafting but the presence of small-scale and expedient crafting of bone artifacts is clear from other Yinxu contexts, some of which may have taken place in domestic settings (Li 2019; Campbell et al. 2022). It is also likely that there were other, less archaeologically visible, cottage industries such as basket and textile weaving and wood working.

2.2.2 Rural Non-elites: Guandimiao, Xingyang

Beyond Yinxu, the village site of Guandimiao offers a rural comparison to Xiaomintun's urban non-elites. Located 200 km southwest of Yinxu near the former Shang capital of Zhengzhou, Guandimiao is the best-preserved Shang village site excavated to date (Figure 1). Originally nearly three ha in size, three quarters of the original Shang site remained to be excavated, revealing 22 houses, 32 wells, 228 tombs, and 1,472 middens as well as storage and sacrificial pits (Li, Campbell, and Hou 2018). In addition, twenty-three pottery kilns were excavated along with abundant ceramic production tools and waste suggesting that Guandimiao was a village of potters. The close correspondence of the number of kilns to that of houses and in some cases, their spatial proximity, suggests that the basic unit of pottery production was also the household. Whether or not production was organized at a higher scale is unclear at present but is the focus of current research.

In addition to ceramic production, zooarchaeological work has shown that pigs, dogs, and cattle, but very few caprines (less than 4 percent) were raised at the site. This contrasts with Yinxu where sheep and goat make up a larger percentage of the zooarchaeological assemblage and suggests that there was regional diversity in animal husbandry. Despite the rural location of Guandimiao, wild taxa only accounted for about 2–5 percent of the assemblage, which, along with the small number of arrowheads recovered from the site, indicates that hunting was not a major activity. Moreover, if Xiaomintun appears to be on the consumption side of the meat production husbandry model, Guandimiao is its production complement: sex and mortality profiles demonstrate that Guandimiao pigs and possibly cattle were mostly raised for consumption elsewhere (Hou et al. 2019). In other words, whether pottery production or animal husbandry, much of the economic activity of the Guandimiao villagers appears to have been geared toward exchange.

At the same time, the villagers of Guandimiao likely also tended fields and practiced a certain amount of crafting for local use. A bone-working study has revealed that approximately half of the worked bone assemblage recovered from the site was low-effort crafting likely performed by unskilled or semi-skilled workers, some of it expedient tool production, while the other half was the product of either local specialists (oracle-bone preparation) or the products of the large-scale bone workshops of the capital (Hou et al. 2018). This suggests that while the villagers of Guandimiao were clearly integrated into regional and inter-regional economic networks, there was also considerable activity geared toward provisioning local or household needs, especially food production.

All of the Guandimiao residences were small semisubterranean structures 5–7 m^2 in area, similar in size to the single-room houses at Xiaomintun, with hearths but lacking sleeping platforms. This again suggests that the basic unit of the domestic economy was no larger than a nuclear family. A systematic zooarchaeological study comparing bone fragmentation, butchery, cooking vessel, and carcass size as well as the distribution of animal remains came to the conclusion that meals were mostly eaten in small groups, but that the consumption of animals such as pigs or cattle implied some sort of exchange, either via reciprocal sharing or collective rituals (Zhang 2022). The latter hypothesis has the support of the rich ceremonial life of the village evidenced in the ritual deposits including cattle and human sacrifice and the abundance of oracle-bones. The similarities in burial, sacrifice, and divination between Yinxu and Guandimiao strongly suggest that the villagers shared the ancestral paradigm of Shang ritual and thus, lineage organization. It is likely that, as at the capital, sacrifice and lineage ritual was the major mechanism through which large animals such as cattle were consumed (Campbell 2022).

Based on several lines of evidence, the Guandimiao villagers seem impoverished in comparison to non-elites of the capital. Firstly, there were almost no bronze artifacts recovered from the site (one knife, two arrowheads) and studies of bone-working (Hou et al. 2018; Li, Campbell, and Hou 2018) and butchery patterns (Zhang 2022) suggest that bronze tools were rare. Sawing, splitting, cutting, filleting, and harvesting were instead done by stone and shell tools. The zooarchaeological assemblage is likewise small given the excavation area, approximately one-tenth the quantity of animal bones recovered from a similar area at Xiaomintun (Li, Campbell, and Hou 2018). Nevertheless, a stable isotopic study suggests similar levels of nitrogen enrichment in the diets of populations at the two sites (Zhang 2022), and the Guandimiao assemblage was heavily impacted by dogs, meaning that many small and medium animal bones were likely consumed (Hou et al. 2019). The tombs at Guandimiao are nearly without grave goods despite following the basic structural patterns of those at the capital, with waist pits and dog sacrifices and ledges and inner and outer coffins in a few large tombs. Thus, despite clear mortuary hierarchy mimicking the forms of the capital and likely indicating local lineage leaders, the tombs, though unlooted, are equipped with grave goods far poorer than what would be expected of similar tombs at Yinxu (Campbell 2018; Li, Campbell, and Hou 2018). Whether interring a few burial goods was a local custom or simply another manifestation of rural poverty is unclear. At the same time, there is no relative difference in house sizes or associated assemblages and the ceramic assemblage is largely limited to a few practical forms such as cooking tripods, bowls, and large storage jars. If the evidence of poverty is not entirely equivocal, it is nevertheless clear that rural non-elites lacked access to many of the goods and amenities available to non-elites of the capital even if the villagers were also far more economically integrated than the autarkic peasants of prior scholarly imagination.

2.3 Elite Domestic Economies

Like those of commoners, elite domestic economies are not well-understood. The palace-temple district at Yinxu, Anyang was extensively excavated in the early part of the twentieth century by archaeologists who had not yet mastered the difficulties of excavating what are essentially features distinguished merely by different colors and textures of earth. As a result, there continue to be many uncertainties concerning the architectural layout of the palace-temple district or its changes through time (Zhongguo 2003; Campbell 2014). Fortunately, elite residences have been excavated in other areas of Yinxu, giving us a glimpse of how the upper classes may have lived. A cluster of courtyard structures excavated at Beixujiaqiaocun two km south-west of the palace-temple area are hypothesized to be the residences of nonroyal elites and the center of a satellite lineage settlement (Meng and Li 2004). Nearer to the core, in the multi-crafting industrial area of Dasikong (Campbell 2014; Zhongguo 2014), several clusters of houses and tombs were excavated including what has been

Figure 6 Dasikong chariot pit M231 (Kaogu yanjiusuo 2014, plate 115-2).

hypothesized to be the ancestral temple of the local lineage (Figure 5). This hypothesis rests on the presence of elite tombs and chariot pits buried beneath its foundations (Figure 6), and the abundant foundation urn burials. At the same time, however, the cluster includes many buildings as well as wells and sewage pipes suggesting that at least some of the buildings may have had a residential function.

Many of the houses in the Dasikong clusters were much smaller than the more than 1,000 m^2 putative palace-temple complex of the lineage leaders, ranging down to houses in the 10 m^2 range. While the 2004 excavations did not recover evidence of large-scale craft production, previous excavations uncovered evidence of bronze casting and large-scale bone-working (Campbell 2014; Li 2019). Given the spatial proximity of the residential and burial groups to the crafting areas, it is probable that the residents of the Dasikong clusters were involved in craft production. At the same time, the artifacts recovered from the residential areas show little evidence of domestic crafting beyond the spindle whorls, antler arrowheads, bone awls, spades and spatulas, stone adzes and axes, and stone and shell blades (usually identified as "sickles") and expedient tools of various shapes and materials typical of Shang residential assemblages everywhere. A preliminary interpretation of these domestic tools assemblages is that they are evidence of a range of general domestic activities that a wide segment of the population took part in that likely included basic weaving, sewing, building, carpentry, food preparation, garden or field planting, tending, and harvesting, pit digging, basket weaving and so on. Which of these activities were organized collectively and which were organized individually or in family groups requires further study.

A unique cache of oracle-bone inscriptions discovered on the outskirts of the palace-temple area at Yinxu reveals aspects of the estate economy of a prince (Schwartz 2013; Cao 2014). Turtle plastrons and cattle scapula were received from subordinates and inventoried, human and animal sacrifices were presented to spirits and ancestors, and gifts were given and received to and from superiors, allies, and inferiors. Gifted items included jades, salt, cowrie shells, and slaves. At the same time, the prince employed traders and traded horses and metal. The prince divined about feasting, dancing and sacrificing, hosting the king and queen, hunting, war, and building a palace – all of which employed unknown numbers of slaves as well as various types of retainers and consumed large numbers of livestock, people, and game as well as quantities of spiced wine, salt, and grain. The image that emerges is of a wealth economy focused on ritual and status – one that is similar to that of the king, but smaller in scale. If craft production and agriculture were a part of this princely economy it is not clear from his divinations. It is possible that these activities were associated with the prince's estate and certainly his feasts and sacrifices had to have been provisioned somehow, but the management of basic provisioning was apparently not a matter that required his divination.

Land tenure, labor organization, and the nature of property in general are difficult topics and the degree to which ordinary households owned property individually or collectively within their lineage is not entirely clear. While it is likely that the products of small-scale and domestic crafting were for household or individual consumption, it is clear that large-scale industries like bronze casting and some bone artifact production were organized at a higher scale. As will be discussed in greater depth in the next section, commoners were mobilized by the king for war, labor, and agriculture, suggesting that if the analogy holds for lesser elites as well, low-ranking lineage members might have worked the fields of their lineage leaders, assisting with building their projects and following them to war. The degree to which they also had their own fields or to which land was owned by the lineage and they were provisioned via redistributive mechanisms is not clear. Whatever the general answer to that question is, urban and rural dwellers were certainly different. The craftspeople of Yinxu's great workshops were not full-time farmers and the urban population was not self-sufficient in terms of food. It is evident that most of the individual urban households did not possess much if any land or livestock. Rural commoners, however, like those at Guandimiao, did possess agricultural assets and at least their craft production and consumption seemed to be based on single-family households. From the perspective of elites, the evident mobility and wealth of some meant that they had both urban residences and rural estates. The wealth they consumed was acquired via trade, booty, tribute, and gifting but also regularized extractions from subordinate lineage members, as well as conquered and enslaved populations supplying labor in their fields and construction projects.

3 Institutional Economy

In a sense, the largest economic institution of the Shang kingdom was the polity itself. At the same time, it is difficult to determine the degree to which there was actually a "state economy" as opposed to a (royal) "estate economy" that was similar to those of other elites but greater in scale. On the one hand, this question relates to the degree to which the Shang kingdom was merely a hegemony organized on segmentary principles and the degree to which there were overarching institutions at the level of the polity. On the other hand, it relates to whether the Shang king's household economy was conceptually or factually separate from that of the polity. We know, for instance, that the distinction between the kings' and "state" finances was blurry until quite late in the Western Zhou (Li 2008) but at the same time that there is no reason to believe that, despite strong continuities, Zhou and Shang polity or economy were exactly the same. There is, moreover, debate in the literature concerning the degree of centralization that existed in the Late Shang kingdom, with strong bureaucratic institutions and a centralized economy imagined by some scholars (Li 2019), while others see it as a decentralized hegemony with the king and his lineage merely the most powerful of the many elite lineages ruling over North China (Campbell 2018). These issues have obvious ramifications for understanding the economy at the level of the polity.

3.1 Polity Finance

Archaeologically, the immense size of Yinxu, with its large population, major workshops, elite residences, and the scale of its ritual, raises the question of provisioning. Simply in terms of bulk goods like grain, timber, and fuel, The Great Settlement Shang would have required a massive catchment area and the large-scale movement of goods and, or, people (Campbell 2022; Campbell et al. 2022). Like all major Central Plains settlements Yinxu was located along a river and while there was cattle traction and ox carts (Li et al. 2014), the massive concentration of population, industry, and ritual in the Great Settlement must have entailed huge transportation costs (Campbell 2022). These provisioning needs would have required large-scale storage and transportation infrastructure and a large bureaucracy to manage if they were centrally organized. Recent work at Yinxu has uncovered roads and possibly a canal (there is debate about its dating) (Jing et al. 2013), but no large grain storage facilities though oracle-bone inscriptions record their existence at various locations Figure 5). Against the centralized economy model are the multiple redundant workshops and industrial areas, the apparent division of the site into lineage settlement clusters, and the general image of the Shang polity as a hegemonic polity ruling directly and indirectly over a shifting network of allies and subordinates (Keightley 1983; Campbell 2009, 2018; Lin 2019). Moreover, as argued in the first section and elsewhere (Campbell et al. 2022), there is little evidence of political-economic centralization before or immediately after the Late Shang, this being rather a trait of the Eastern Zhou territorial polities and early empires of the Qin and Han which produced the transmitted textual accounts so influential in Chinese archaeology.

The picture that emerges from the royal oracle-bone divinatory inscriptions is one of kings mostly concerned with ritual, war, and the hunt – all dangerous and uncertain endeavors requiring the approval if not the assistance of the spirits (Keightley 2000; Fiskesjö 2001; Campbell 2018). It is perhaps not surprising then that the economic information that can be gleaned from the oracle-bone inscriptions mostly concerns the ritual economy. Oracle-bone materials were inventoried and divinations were made about tribute and the requisition of various things. Among the things "brought" by subordinates, allies, and occasionally enemies, cattle and captives were the most numerous – paralleling their frequent use in divinations concerning sacrifice (Campbell 2018). Nevertheless, even if the king's divinatory concerns were largely focused on war, hunting, and ritual, the polity or even just the royal household were not provisioned on oracle-bones and sacrificial victims alone.

From the perspective of staple finance, the oracle-bones reveal that the king was directly involved in planting and harvesting activities, praying for harvest, levying labor, and directing or delegating the organization of planting. At the same time, the places where these activities occurred were a small subset of the place names occurring in the oracle-bone divinations (Campbell 2021b). Moreover, these locations were all highly correlated with royal activity and strongly affiliated with the king (Campbell 2018). The king also inspected or ordered the inspection of granaries at various places but never divined about the grain or its transportation. An exception that proves the rule is an inscription that divines about receiving the harvest of Long (a peripheral polity sometimes at war with the Shang) while the king was in the southern colony(ies) (Campbell

2018: 126). Conquered enemy populations were sometimes relocated to colonies (Qiu 1993) and it is possible this had happened to Long or that Long was forced to pay tribute in grain to the king when he visited. In any case, these lines of evidence taken together suggest the existence of royal agricultural estates and colonies scattered across the landscape, but no centralized polity-level staple economy.

Animal husbandry, however, shows a different pattern. There are very few inscriptions that can be interpreted as concerning the management of the king's herds, but numerous inscriptions about the acquisition of livestock via tribute, gifting, requisition, or levy. Significantly, this pattern includes cattle, sheep, and dogs but excludes pigs despite the fact the latter were sometimes used in royal sacrifice and were one of the most common meat sources (Campbell 2022). This suggests that pigs were consumed closer to where they were raised, while cattle, sheep, and dogs circulated in wider provisioning networks. It further suggests royal livestock provisioning from diverse sources.

In general, the pattern for things mobilized or requisitioned is that they focus on those with low transportation costs relative to their worth such as humans and bovids and high-value materials. In fact, large-scale human labor is a conspicuous aspect of Shang polity finance – people were levied in the hundreds or thousands for purposes mostly relating to agriculture or war. These lines of evidence, taken together with the existence of subordinate lords and allies with their own lands and settlements, suggest a mosaic of royal estates and colonies interspersed with those of other elites each with their own granaries and for which labor was levied from local populations. This further suggests that grain itself was not transported long distances but consumed in place and that taxation was largely in terms of mobile things such as labor and livestock.

Another aspect of royal finance is the frequent movement of the king and his entourage across the landscape. While this travel was often to royal estates, the king also visited subordinates and allies, conducting rituals, hunts, and warfare (Keightley 2000). The political and ritual aspects of this royal movement have been often noted but the economic ramifications are less commented on. As in similar institutions in other societies such as Hawaii (Kirch 2012) or Anglo-Saxon England (Crabtree 2018) the moving court had the dual economic advantages of defraying the costs of maintaining the royal entourage while also reducing the need for expensive taxation infrastructure. In general, the patterns of royal extraction as seen in the oracle-bones suggest a system that minimized transportation costs, mobilized labor, and levied livestock and other easily transportable things. As in economies like that of the Inca, the major mode of extraction appears to be in terms of labor rather than taxation in kind

(D'Altroy 2009). There is, however, no evidence of polity-level managed agriculture or redistribution mechanisms as opposed to those focused on provisioning the estates of the king and other elites. Polity-level extractive mechanisms may have only included royal visits with their associated rituals, feasting, and gifting as well as levies of labor and livestock – in other words, upscaled and hierarchically subverted versions of basic lineage institutions of reciprocity and redistribution. The only positive evidence of any sort of taxation in kind comes from a unique bronze inscription from the end of the dynasty (Xiao Chen Yue Fang Ding) that records the royal gifting of five years of the income / harvests of Yu to an aristocratic subordinate (Ma 1986: 7). This implies that income derived from a territory could be conceived as separate from its rulership as well as of fixed duration though it is still not clear how portable that income was, how the "yields" were extracted or even what form they took.

3.2 Elite Estates

As mentioned in the previous section, Shang elites had their own estate economies mirroring those of the king in lesser form. The oracle-bone inscriptions record allies and subordinate lords with their own lands, fields, and people. The distribution of what are sometimes called "clan insignia" on Shang ritual bronzes is often interpreted in terms of the distribution of elite lineages and their subdivisions. While controversy remains over the exact nature of these signs (Zhu 1990; Tang 2004; Cao 2018), that they generally relate to elite group insignia is not controversial. Their distribution reveals networks of elites across North China, clustering in cemeteries of the capital as well as those much further afield. This pattern suggests kin networks that crossed large distances and, or, elites that, like the king, possessed multiple estates.

3.3 Large-Scale Workshops

Another economic institution of the Late Shang is the large workshops located in and around the Great Settlement. As noted in the first section, there is a relationship between elite centers and certain forms of craft production that go back at least to the Erlitou period. While this phenomenon may have had its origin in palace provisioning, by the Late Shang this was no longer the case. As will be discussed in greater detail in the next section, there are workshops associated with the palace-temple area and crafting that is only associated with the highest elites (Li 2019), but the largest workshops were focused on or also produced goods used by a wider spectrum of the population than just high elites (eg. bronze weapons and tools, bone hairpins, etc.). The two archaeologically visible examples are bone and bronze workshops, but it is possible there were others. While some authors argue that these were "state workshops," their multiple locations, redundant production and the lineage settlement cluster interpretation of the Great Settlement argue against this perspective. At the same time, the concentration of this sort of large-scale production in the capital and its lack of evidence elsewhere argues for some sort of centripetal mechanism. A major concern of Shang kings was the control of people, but, at the same time, there was no indication of strong mechanisms of central administration such as that existed in the Qin and Han empires. The evidence of bureaucracy is at best equivocal with aristocratic agents performing a wide range of functions. There is a category of retainer termed "the many artisans" (*duo gong*) which might have indicated a set of officials responsible for industry and construction, but since they largely appear in ritual contexts in the oracle-bones it is difficult to determine their status or the scope of their responsibilities. Based on the palace/estate economy model that has been constructed thus far, it seems likely that they were retainers/officials serving the royal household. Whatever ties or incentives cajoled or coerced the numerous elite lineages to settle in the capital, the location of the great workshops there makes a great deal of economic sense. Yinxu was 100 times larger than any other known Shang site of its time and the cultic and political center of the Shang world. It was where the consumers were, and at least in the case of the bone workshops, where the raw materials were as well. If, as most scholars believe, each craft or even multi-crafting industrial area was managed by an elite lineage, then it seems likely that, as in later times, craft production and resource extraction was a source of revenue for the families that controlled them. This hypothesis is corroborated in the case of the large bone-working sites where the conjunction of abundant raw materials, consumers, skilled craftspeople, economies of scale, and technological innovation led to a quantum leap in efficiency that in turn resulted in a focus on the mass production of high-value-added products like hairpins. In other words, the advent of large-scale bone-working appears to have been motivated by the maximization of profit. The model of lineages specializing in particular trades also fits the evidence of non-elite settlements and the deep-time pattern of resource-dependent regional specialization (Campbell et al. 2022). If this is so, then lineages, elite and common, producing crafts and extracting resources for exchange, were a major structural element of the Shang economy.

3.4 Ritual Economy

Ritual was a major component of elite and non-elite activity. Specifically, divination, feasting, sacrifice, burial, and other rites were aimed at the avoidance or amelioration of spiritual disfavor, the maintenance of proper relations between the various constituents of the Shang world, and, in general, the generation of auspicious outcomes. These concerns were widely shared and were woven through the most fundamental aspects of Shang life from eating to social relations to the burial of the dead. What remains to us in the archaeological record is dominated by these practices – the palace-temples, sacrificial grounds, and monumental tombs of the elites, the tens of thousands of turtle plastrons and cattle scapula used in royal divination, and the thousands of tons of ritual bronzes cast. Even for the relatively impoverished villagers of Guandimiao, much of their consumption of resources – from oracle-bones to sacrificial pits to burials – was related to ritual concerns. Indeed, long before the term "ritual economy" was popularized in archaeological theory (eg. Wells 2008), K.C. Chang argued for the importance of ritual in the constitution of the Shang civilization (Chang 1983). Although more recent research has painted a more complex and encompassing picture than Chang's shamanistic elite monopoly model (Campbell 2018), the fundamental point about the importance of ritual to Shang life and its economy remains valid.

The most frequently commented upon aspect of the Shang ritual economy since K. C. Chang's seminal works was the bronze industry. At least four major bronze workshops were in simultaneous operation at Yinxu (Li 2019) with tens of thousands of ceramic molds recovered, mostly for ritual bronze vessels, giving mute testimony to their importance. Over a ton of cast metal was excavated from the tomb of one queen, while another was buried with a bronze cauldron weighing over 800 kg (Chang 1983) (Figure 7). One study has conservatively estimated that a thousand tons of bronze was cast in the Yinxu workshops into more than 100,000 vessels consuming millions of hours of skilled labor. This, in turn, would have required hundreds of thousands of tons of fuel, all of which had to be transported. The metal itself – tin, copper and lead – was mined and smelted in a variety of locations, with some of the known sources beyond the plausible reach of direct control (Campbell 2013). A recent discovery of a cache of nearly 3.5 metric tons of lead ingots of various provenience near one of the foundries gives evidence of both the scale and diverse sources of the Yinxu metal industry (Anyang Work Team, Institute of Archaeology, CASS 2018). As ritual bronze vessels were central to elite ancestral sacrificial rites and burials, and Shang kingship itself predicated on the king's role as lineage leader of the world, the production and distribution of bronze vessels was a key aspect of Shang political economy.

Another less frequently noted aspect of the ritual economy was the sacrificial offerings themselves. In royal sacrifice, the most common of these included humans, cattle, sheep/goats, pigs, and dogs as well as grain and millet wine. In some major rituals, hundreds of offerings could be made, but with rituals

Figure 7 Shang bronze vessel: the Simu Wu rectangular *ding*-cauldron. (Allan 2005, figure 6.22).

occurring at frequent intervals, if not daily, the total cost of royal ritual must have been immense. The provisioning of sacrifice was the major economic concern divined about in the oracle-bone inscriptions. Nevertheless, the economic implications of the different rituals and sacrificial offerings were not the same. Sacrifices involving burning, burying, or drowning for instance, completely removed the offering from human consumption, while rituals involving feasting effectively functioned as food redistribution mechanisms. At the same time, while humans are the most common form of sacrificial victim in royal sacrifice, there is no direct evidence of cannibalism. Indeed, in comparison to their frequency in the oracle-bone divinations, nonhuman offerings are suspiciously underrepresented in sacrificial pits, suggesting that the meat of most sacrificial animals was shared among the living, a tradition that continues down to today (Chang 1980; Li and Campbell 2019).

There are several indirect lines of evidence that suggest that the consumption of large animals like cattle was mostly or entirely derived from sacrificial rites

Figure 8 Ceramic *Li*-tripod from Guandimiao (image courtesy of the Henan Institute of Cultural Heritage and Archaeology).

and feasting events. The first is simply the size of the animals and the hundreds of kilograms of meat one head of cattle represents. While drying, salting and smoking might have accounted for some of the meat, much of it was likely cooked for feasting events or shared out and consumed at home. A study of animal carcass processing at Xiaomintun, Anyang has shown that most cattle and pig meat was cooked bone-in with only moderate evidence of filleting and low intensity of carcass processing performed by specialized butchers with bronze chopping tools (Zhang 2022: 201–2). For smaller cuts, this meant cooking in medium to large li-tripods (Figure 8), while some whole limb bones suggest roasting on the bone (Zhang 2022: 229). All of this suggests that the consumption of cattle was largely in terms of fresh meat. In addition, a zooarchaeological study of non-elite residential areas at Yinxu has shown that cattle overtook pigs by a number of identified specimens in phase III, meaning that even Shang commoners were eating as much or more beef than pork by the latter half of the Late Shang (Li 2009). This picture is confirmed by a recent isotopic study (Cheung et al. 2017: 42) indicating that roughly 25 percent of the dietary protein from all sources and approximately 40 percent of the animal protein of the non-elite sample derived from cattle (herbivores that primarily consumed C-4 plants). A third line of evidence is the scale of the royal sacrifices as well as – based on the model of widely shared analogous ritual practices – the fact that every lineage had ancestors and thus sacrifice and ritual feasting events.

An estimate of the scale of elite sacrifice over the course of the roughly 200 years of the Late Shang reaches over 500,000 head of cattle, 710,000 pigs, and 230,000 sheep (Campbell 2022), while extrapolations from the assemblages of the residential area at Xiaomintun (Li 2009) or the bone-working site of Tiesanlu (Campbell et al. 2011) both arrive at minimum number of individual cattle in the 300,000–400,000 range (Campbell 2022: 99). Given that Shang elites had their own sacrificial economies and MNI is nearly always a low estimate, these estimates are certainly too low, plausibly by several factors. This conclusion is further supported by the fact that the Xiaomintun and Tiesanlu assemblages do not show bone element complementarity and thus the workshop assemblage is not derived from the residential one (Campbell 2022: 99). Taken together, from the scale of sacrificial activities, the relative dearth of animals in sacrificial pits, the huge amounts of cattle consumed, as well as butchery and cooking patterns suggesting fresh consumption, it is highly likely that sacrificial sharing and feasting events redistributed much of the meat consumed at Yinxu, especially beef.

The massive scale of the sacrifice and consumption of cattle at Yinxu also spawned a number of second-order industries such as the huge bone workshops at Tiesanlu, Beixinzhuang, Dasikong, and Huayuanzhuang where cattle bone was the major raw material in the mass production of hairpins and other goods (Li, He, and Jiang 2011). Elite hunting activities, also ritualized behavior, supplied the huge quantities of antlers that were worked into arrowheads, awls, and other artifacts, while the bones, horn, and ivory of more exotic creatures hunted or brought in tribute were crafted into unique prestige goods (Li 2019). The furs, feathers, and hides of various creatures hunted or sacrificed were undoubtedly also manufactured into diverse items though no archaeological evidence remains. Tanning was likely a major second-order industry of the ritual economy but likewise has not been identified archaeologically.

Other partial derivatives of cattle sacrifice were the scapulas and occasional pelvises used in oracle-bone divination (Hou et al. 2018). Keightley estimates that 69,000 cattle scapulas (and 69,000 turtle plastrons) were used in royal divination in the 150 years from kings Wu Ding to Di Xin (assuming a short chronology, or 200 years assuming a long chronology) (Keightley 1985: 169). Given the estimates of cattle consumption at Yinxu and the fact that basically every cattle scapula in a Late Shang site seems to end up as an oracle-bone, oracle-bone scapula should number in the millions for Yinxu alone. The discrepancy between this figure and Keightley's estimate likely indicates that the latter's estimate is too low, that the royal divinations accounted for only a tiny fraction of the total oracle-bone divination at Yinxu, or both. Other scholars have estimated that inscribed royal oracle-bones account for only 10 percent of the total (Flad 2008) but it may have been less than that. In either case, this suggests the importance of nonroyal institutions in the total ritual economy.

On the royal oracle-bones themselves there are records of contributions of oracle-bones, while requisitions of scapulas and especially plastrons are common (Keightley 1985; Campbell 2018). This suggests, that like the offerings of royal sacrifice, royal divination too was provisioned from numerous sources via diverse mechanisms including gifting, tribute, and requisition. By extension, this was likely true of the ritual economies of lesser elites. Another aspect of the economy of divination was the specialist labor it required. While the royal oracle-bones were ritually prepared by diviners and royal wives, sawed, chiseled, drilled, cracked, divined, and then inscribed, even the oracle-bones of commoners in remote villages like Guandimiao show a degree of care and specialization not seen in other categories of local bone-working. If we consider that oracle-bone divination was just the tip of the Shang ritual iceberg then the gargantuan amount of materials, skilled and unskilled labor, as well as specialized knowledge employed in ritual activities begins to emerge.

A final aspect of the Shang ritual economy to be discussed is the cost of human sacrifice. While it could be argued that there was no great cost in sacrificing war captives beyond guarding them during their transportation to the capital and digging the pits where they would be buried, recent studies have suggested that sacrificial victims were kept at Yinxu for years before being killed. This raises the likelihood that there was a substantial population of slaves at Yinxu – minimally sacrificial-livestock-in-waiting but more plausibly a pool of forced labor that was also available for sacrifice. If this is so, then human sacrifice, unlike other sacrificial livestock (except cattle and horses), incurred a huge opportunity cost in lost potential labor. The magnitude of this loss is difficult to determine. A count of divinations about human sacrifice yielded over 10,000 (Hu 1974), while there were an estimated 15,000 human sacrificial victims buried in the palace-temple area and royal cemetery (Campbell 2012, 2018) (Figure 9). This does not include those burned or thrown into the river and is certainly a low estimate. The question is by how much is this estimate off? If Keightley's estimation that only 5 percent of the royal divinations have been recovered is correct, then Hu's count of 10,000 must be multiplied by a factor of 20. This would accord with the estimation of royal cattle sacrifice and the observation human sacrifice appears to be the most common form of offering in the royal inscriptions. If there were on the order of 100,000 human sacrifices at Yinxu, it would simultaneously indicate a huge opportunity cost in labor, while over a 200-year period only amounting to about 500 human sacrifices per year in a population in the hundreds of thousands. Moreover, the practice, which expanded to unprecedented heights in the reign of the warlike Wu Ding,

Figure 9 Shang sacrificial pits in royal cemetery: two pits with human sacrifices, one with a pig (Zhongguo 1994, plate 16).

seems to have tapered off by the end of the dynasty when numerous earlier ritual extravagances were economized (Huang 2004; Jiang 2012; Campbell 2018) and cattle replaced humans as the most common offering.

4 Specialization

Specialization is a broad and complex topic that can be explored at a number of scales. Economic specialization can exist at the scale of regions, between industries, at the community level, as well as in terms of individual economic roles. Other senses of specialization can be relevant for production, such as the degree of specialization in production organization (Costin 1991) or in terms of production output (Campbell et al. 2011; Hou et al. 2018; Wang et al. 2022). In addition to the fact that specialization can mean many things, the degree of specialization can differ within a single industry or institution making generalizations difficult. Nevertheless, properly contextualized, specialization remains a useful perspective for investigating diverse aspects of ancient economies.

4.1 Regional Specialization

At the largest scale, there are numerous lines of evidence that show regional economic specialization. While on some level this is not surprising given the uneven distribution of resources, the existence of regional specialization extending back into at least the third millennium BCE shows a degree of exchange and economic integration that long predated the Late Shang. A late first millennium BCE text refers to the tribute given to a legendary ruler with each region sending in different offerings (Underhill and Fang 2004). While clearly there is much that is anachronistic in the text, both the range of goods and how few of them would have been preserved archaeologically is noteworthy. Thus, though lacquer, silk, salt, hemp cloth, rare birds, different types of wood, leather, feathers, and fruits are more difficult to identify archaeologically than bronze or jade buried in tombs, they are useful reminders both of what is missing from the archaeological record and the potential economic role of different regions when linked together in exchange networks.

From an archaeological perspective, there was specialized salt production in Shanxi and the coastal regions of Shangdong, copper mines in Anhui, Jiangxi and Hunan, stoneware was imported from the Yangzi region, lustrous stones (dolomite, nephrite, etc.) were mined in the mountains of Shanxi but also widely believed to have come from as far away as Xinjiang, while some cowries shells came from as far as the Indian Ocean (Campbell et al. 2022). Turquoise and cinnabar were likewise only available in certain regions. The zooarchaeology atced hairpins were only produced in the capital but consumed widely in the Shang kingdom. From a large-scale perspective then, the Shang economy linked and was linked to networks of specialized production and exchange that stretched throughout and beyond East Asia. This was especially true of prestige goods, but even major industries like bronze casting, livestock husbandry, stone, bone and shell tool production, salt processing, and possibly even ceramic production were regionally or locally specialized. Following the logic of minimizing transportation costs, raw materials like ores, brine, or stone were first smelted, processed, or turned into blanks at or near their sites of extraction before exchange. In the case of relatively low value to bulk industries like stone tool or pottery production, the product may have been finished at the primary production site, but for more complex technologies such as metallurgy, the mining and smelting sites were often distant from the final casting sites.

The pattern of regional or local specialization by product thus differed depending on the industry. In the case of high-skill, prestige good-focused crafting like bronze casting, ivory, and fine bone carving, the final production was generally concentrated in the capital. The distances involved and the number of spatially segregated stages from resource to finished product depended on the craft, but at one end of the spectrum bronze casting could involve diverse communities and raw materials from beyond the Shang kingdom, long-distance transportation, and then multiple discreet and complex tasks at the foundries of the capital (Li 2019). On the other end of the spectrum, bone, antler stone, or shell fragments could be expediently worked into tools in a completely standalone process.

4.2 Division of Labor and Professional Specialization

From the perspective of the role of the division of labor in economic integration, evidence for non-prestige good specialization takes on special significance. While the focus on bronze casting and other prestige good industries had encouraged the image of the Shang as an elite wealth economy sitting atop a base of self-sufficient villages utilizing technologies unchanged since the Neolithic (Chang 1983), the fact that every small Chinese Bronze Age site excavated thus far seems to have a specialized economic function argues against this perspective. Ceramic production and animal husbandry are two industries that, based on prior assumptions, should be ubiquitous and self-sufficient in Shang villages. The village site of Guandimiao, however, shows that was not true of either industry as ceramics were produced and livestock were raised largely for exchange. In some ways, this is a ramification of the pattern where raw materials are processed at the site of their abundance – this would logically imply that communities specialized in one task would have to acquire their other goods from somewhere else. In the case of Guandimiao, while it is unlikely that its ceramics or pigs traveled long distances, its cattle may have, a significant portion of its bone artifacts was produced in the capital, its few bronze artifacts were certainly not made locally and even its shell and stone tools were exogenous. All this strongly indicates that in addition to regional and inter-regional specialization in prestige goods production and exchange, economic specialization existed at the level of the community as well and included many of the most common items of consumption.

The hypothesis that craft production in the Shang kingdom was kinship-based has a long pedigree. This hypothesis was originally based on interpretations of later texts that recount the deportation of various lineages of the defeated Shang people by the Zhou whose lineage names are generally interpreted to be occupation-related: potters, rope-makers, bridle makers, etc. (Chang 1980: 231). The insignia on Shang bronzes have also been interpreted as indicating professions (Chang 1980; Cao 2018), though this is not a universally accepted hypothesis. Another line of evidence, if circumstantial, combines the lineage-based nature of Shang society with the location of particular crafts – if the Great Settlement is a cluster of discrete lineage settlements, then the location of certain crafts within some settlements, but not others, supports specialization at the lineage level.

There is, however, also evidence that mitigates professional specialization in many contexts. Elites, for instance, although possibly serving different professional roles, were elites by merit of the status of their lineage and, or, place within it. Shang elites shared a common basis of authority in their practices of warfare, ritual, hunting, and divination (Chang 1983; Keightley 2000). The tombs of elites mark status in relatively codified ways that revolve around implements of ritual and war (Campbell 2018). Prominent actors in the oracle-bone inscriptions that perform economic actions such as bringing in captives and cattle, or organizing agricultural activities also conduct rituals, lead forces in battle and join hunts. The "many artisans" (*duo gong*) of royal inscriptions are mostly seen performing rituals (Li 2019). Shang elite education almost certainly included chariot-riding, archery, ritual (including sacrifice, music, and dance), divination, and likely hand-to-hand combat as well. The leaders of economically specialized lineages, as Shang elites, would have been no different, and indeed, this is what is reflected in elite mortuary assemblages, even in craft production areas like Dasikong (Zhongguo 2014). Nevertheless, even if elite status was associated with certain practices and the principal actors of the oracle-bone inscriptions seem to perform a variety of functions, it does not mean that lower-ranking lineages or lineage members were not more specialized or at least had a main profession or role in addition to their other duties. This is evident in the oracle-bone diviners that Shang kings employed despite being able to conduct divinations themselves. It can also be seen in the fact that the oracle-bones used at the village of Guandimiao were clearly prepared by a local specialist (Hou et al. 2018), or that animal butchery patterns at Yinxu indicate the presence of professional butchers (Zhang 2022).

There were different degrees of specialization both within some workshops and between particular forms of crafting within the same industry. In the first case, complex processes like bronze casting involved a number of tasks of differing complexity and requiring different degrees and types of skill. These included making the multicomponent ceramic molds and models, melting and mixing the metal, pouring the molten mixture into the prepared mold, and finally grinding off the mold marks. For some objects, like ritual bronzes, intricate designs and even inscriptions had to be added to the molds and, or, models. Studies of bronze casting organization at the Yinxu foundries have argued that a division of labor existed between crafters carrying out different production steps and of different technical difficulties (Li 2019). A similarly multistep production process is also apparent in the case of the large-scale bone workshops of Yinxu, with evidence of discrete areas for different stages, production in batches, and quality control (Campbell et al. 2011).

4.2.1 Bone Crafting

For variation in specialization within the same industry, bone crafting provides the best example. There were multiple forms or modes of Shang bone-working (Campbell et al. 2011; Hou et al. 2018; Wang et al. 2022). Earlier at sites such as Erlitou or Zhengzhou there seems to be two modes of bone crafting – small-scale workshops producing a wide range of goods and domestic, expedient production. The former was mostly formal and ran a spectrum from high-investment prestige goods to everyday tools. The later was mostly informal and focused on ad hoc modification of bone fragments for expedient uses. The small, formal workshops may have been elite-sponsored or at least patronized, but there is little evidence that they exclusively served elites (Campbell et al. 2022). This situation changed during the Late Shang. On the one hand, Li Yung-ti argues for the existence of a workshop associated with the palace-temple area focused on the production of unique, "hypertrophic," artifacts in ivory or exotic animal bone that have only been recovered from royal tombs (Figure 10) (Li 2019). On the other hand, large-scale bone workshops appear for the first time at Yinxu. These are distinguished from previous and contemporary forms of bone-working in several ways. The first is scale. A ten- meter-wide trench through the bone workshop at Tiesanlu produced over thirty-four metric tons of animal bone waste and it was estimated that the large-scale bone workshops at Yinxu produced millions of artifacts (Campbell et al. 2011). The second characteristic is the standardization of raw materials – artifact types were produced from a narrow range of specific high-quality taxa, elements, and parts. A third distinguishing characteristic is the standardization of production steps – artifacts of the same type were produced in the same way and initial blank reduction steps were shared across similar artifact classes. A final distinguishing characteristic is the ubiquitous use of specialized tools including bronze saws and pump drills. These were essentially proto-factories mass-producing high-value-added artifacts for broad consumption (Campbell et al. 2011, 2022). Replication experiments have shown that bronze saws made working thick bone – the preferred material for hairpins, some awls, sturdy spatulas, and combs – orders of magnitude more efficient than other potential tools (Wang et al. 2022). These saws and their characteristic marks have only been discovered at Yinxu for this period. The dramatic increase in efficiency allowed the mass production of artifact types that previously required hours of tedious labor to craft. As a result, the Yinxu bone-working industry stratified, with small-scale workshops or part-time specialists still plying their trade but focusing on things not produced in the large workshops, or for which the absence of saws was less of a comparative disadvantage – such as bone blades, spatulas, needles and awls made from thinner bone such as ribs or fragments that required less modification. Small-scale specialist bone-working is

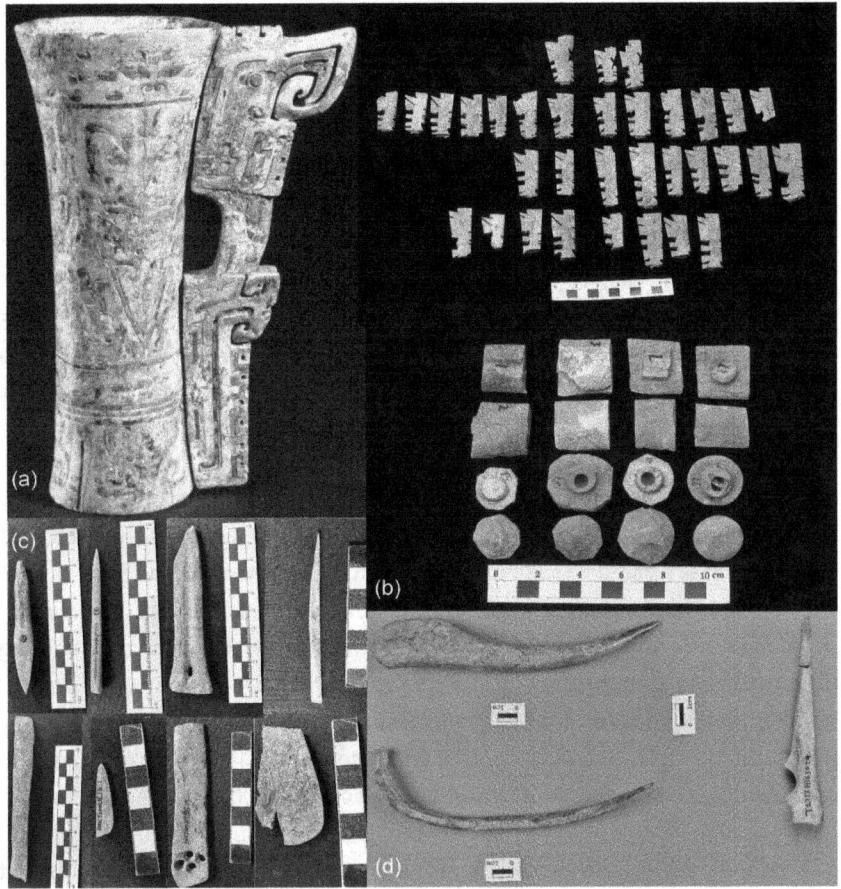

Figure 10 Shang bone-working. (a) Hypertrophic turquoise inlaid ivory cup from the tomb of queen Fu Hao (Shijie 2008, fig. 48, pp. 169). (b) Tiesanlu bone workshop hairpin head wasters in different production stages (after Campbell et al. 2011, fig. 10). (c) Daxinzhuang small-scale bone-working (photograph by author). (d) Guandimiao expedient bone-working (after Hou et al. 2018, fig. 3).

characterized by the presence of some specialized tool use (chisels, drills, knives, but not saws), a greater degree of skill/labor investment than ad hoc production, and a heterogeneity of materials, products, and methods. Finally, the existence of the ad hoc production of expedient tools continued as barely modified fragments were sometimes used as awls, hammers, or other tools.

While each industry and each type of product within it had its own significance in terms of relations of production, exchange, and consumption, the bone-working industry can be used as a window into at least some of those relations at Yinxu. The small-scale palace-temple area bone workshop was part of a multi-crafting area that included lapidary, bronze, shell, marble, and possibly lacquer and carpentry workshops (Li 2019: 129–63) – partially analogous to the multi-crafting areas at Beixinzhuang-Xiaomintun, Tiesanlu-Miaopu north, and Dasikong (Figure 5). The reason it is only partially analogous is due to the smaller scale and focus on high-investment crafting. Each of the multi-crafting areas outside of the palace-temple area had a large-scale bone workshop focused on the efficient production of widely used but labor-intensive artifacts, especially hairpins. Small-scale crafting produced the remainder of the formal bone artifacts at Yinxu, while at other Shang sites, like Daxinzhuang, small-scale specialist crafting continued to produce a spectrum of artifacts (Wang et al. 2022). Expedient crafting was widespread but always a minority within bone assemblages even in villages like Guandimiao.

The hypertrophic artifacts of the palace-temple workshops were exclusively produced for the highest elites. While the location of production and restriction of consumption is clear, the relationship between the craftspeople and their patrons is not. Some ritually charged bone-working, like the preparation of oracle-bones was conducted by diviners and royal wives – analogous to Mayan elite crafting (Inomata 2001) – but there is otherwise no evidence that Shang elites participated in other crafting activities directly. Given the high skill and small scale of the work, it is possible, that like the diviners (whose names often correspond with place names), the kings drew the most talented crafters to their palace workshops. Again, analogous to divination with its multiple scribal groups and the evidence of hereditary professions among lower elites and commoners, it is possible that even these royal workshops employed crafting lineages. The royal diviners and scribes are perhaps the best examples of high-skill specialists working in bone and show that, at least for the production of some prestigious things, the provisioning of services to the highest elites did not imply low status.

The location of large-scale workshops producing a wide range of goods in three or four (if we count the wider metropolitan area) industrial areas, suggests a different set of relationships than that of the palace-temple crafters. While Li Yung-ti (Li 2019: 166–67) has argued that the existence of large crafting areasmeans that the "precincts were operating at or above the community level in terms of the sources of labour," and that this, together with the putative royal control of raw materials, implies top-down management, other interpretations are more plausible. Firstly, there is no evidence that the raw materials utilized by the great bone workshops were controlled by the king. In fact, the large number of cattle sacrificed and consumed at Yinxu by lineage elites as well as the king argue against a centralized as opposed to a segmentary or opportunistic sourcing of bone. Moreover, given the low intensity of bone fat utilization (Zhang 2022), it is possible most post-consumption cattle bone (except scapula) was not considered valuable. Finally, the fact that animal bone is widely distributed across the site of Yinxu and utilized in a number of crafting contexts argues strongly against any such centralized resource control. The assumptions that, one, there was an overarching management of the craft precincts and, two, these were too large to be organized around lineages are likewise both problematic. The first is unsupported by any evidence – the industrial areas could just as easily be a collection of independent or allied crafters. The second assumption forgets that the entire Shang kingdom was organized around lineages (Chang 1980; Zhu 1990; Keightley 2000; Campbell 2018) – segmentary or hierarchical kinship structures are easily scalable. An alternative model more in keeping with the evidence is that each workshop (and it is currently unclear if Tiesanlu or Xiaomintun was one or more workshops) was under the control of an internally hierarchical lineage. Based on mortuary evidence, the leaders of these lineages belonged to a Shang elite or lesser elite stratum, responsible for leading their lineage rituals and divination as well as production activities (Campbell 2018). Lower-ranking lineage members would have been assigned tasks according to their skill and ability. Below rank-and-file lineage members, there were likely other categories of dependent laborers, including slaves. While genetic studies would give us a better idea of the degree of relatedness among Shang burial communities, multiple lines of indirect evidence support the idea that elite lineages had numerous dependents not necessarily biologically related to them. These include the practice of the taking of war captives, deportation, retainer sacrifice, royal divinations about taking or bringing various categories of people, the analogy of the assignation of followers to newly established lords in the Western Zhou bronze inscriptions, and finally the fact that Shang lineages were externally as well as internally hierarchical. The large numbers of defeated, enslaved, or otherwise subordinated people, not to mention the generally hierarchical nature of Shang society, imply many different opportunities for the creation of dependencies, ranging from allegiance, patron-client to master-slave and from individuals, families to entire lineages. At this point, however, it is impossible to do more than conjecture based on general models of Shang society.

In contrast to the large-scale workshops, the small-scale wide-spectrum mode of bone tool production was likely to have been practiced by part-time specialist individuals or small groups, perhaps also working materials like wood. These could either have been members of lineages specialized in some other profession who provided basic bone artifacts for their kin, or they could have been independent urban craft producers crafting objects for whoever paid them.

4.3 Status and Economic Roles

Status in the Shang was fundamentally predicated on lineage – both an individual's place among kin and the place of their lineage among others. Ancestral status structured relations between elites and non-elites as well as the living and the dead (Keightley 2004; Campbell 2016). Kinship provided the idiom in which society was reproduced but also organized and naturalized hierarchies in major practices of authority such as warfare, sacrifice, and feasting. It is therefore likely that lineage status was also a major element in the division of labor at Yinxu. If Shang lineage elites shared common ritual obligations and practices, low-ranking lineage members (and low-ranking lineages) likely did the majority of the actual labor. Dependents assimilated or attached to the lineage as servants or slaves were likewise likely present in major lineages but the nature and extent of these practices is murky. Above the households of elite lineages, but probably originally derived from their internal divisions of labor, the Shang kings employed a number of retainers, emissaries, and functionaries. Where the identities of these officials can be reconstructed, they are generally seen to be aristocrats themselves – representatives of other elite lineages if not royal kin. Most of these functionaries seem to perform a variety of roles in the oracle-bone inscriptions as befits their status as elites. The general categories in the formula of "the many X," however, signify collectives of variable statuses. These include "the horse keepers" (lit. the many horses), "the dog keepers," "the archers," "the officers," "the slave/barbarians (keepers)" and "the artisans." While the exact nature of any of these groups is unclear (at least in part due to the particularities of royal divination) they do show that there were distinct categories of people that served the king in particular roles, some of whom were of low status. Keightley (Keightley 2012: 45) interprets the wide range of activities of the artisans (and other categories of functionary) as corresponding "to what we know about the unspecialized nature of Shang officialdom in general; administrative jurisdictions, in both Shang and Western Zhou, were flexible and broad." I would instead argue that the fact that some of the functionaries, such as "the artisans" (or *Gong*-officers) appear participating in rituals is in keeping with the principal concerns of the oracle-bone inscriptions and with the inseparability of "ritual" from important doings in the Shang and in many other societies as well (Fowles 2013). The putative participation of "artisans" in war is likewise based on a small number of inscriptions with alternate interpretations, making Keightley's claims concerning their generalist role shaky at best. The fact that other categories, like "the dog handlers/many dogs," "the archers" and "the horse handlers/many horse" – which better fit the divinatory foci of the oracle-bones, such as hunting and war – also show a closer and narrower relation between name and function, argues against the view that Shang functionaries lacked specialized roles.

There have long been debates about the existence and extent of Shang slavery. Influenced by Marxism, some twentieth-century mainland Chinese scholars argued that the Shang was a slave society, but most scholarship has swung back against the view that slaves were a large part of the Shang economy. Tang Jigen, based on an estimate of human remains in middens, claimed that slaves accounted for less than 5 percent of the population (Tang 2004), while Keightley argued that Shang labor was fundamentally based on corvee rather than slavery (Keightley 2012). The evidence from the oracle-bone inscriptions is contested with a spectrum of interpretations concerning the status of a variety of terms. The *zhong* (lit. "masses" or "group") has been interpreted as meaning everything from "slaves" to "lesser elites," but most scholars, seeing the term as a unique category of person rather than a general reference to groups, understand them to be a class of slightly higher than commoner status dependents called upon by the king to perform a variety of tasks (Keightley 2012). Due to the fact that the *zhong* (lit. "masses") largely overlap with *ren* ("people") in being mobilized for agriculture and war, I do not believe they represent a distinct category of dependent as opposed to being just a general collective term. Another contested term is *qiang*, interpreted by most as an enemy ethnic group, but also referring to a type of human sacrifice, a class of functionaries and possibly slaves (Shelach 1996; Campbell 2018). Despite the controversy, from the perspective of the division of labor, the few inscriptions that refer to *qiang* outside of being the objects of warfare, capture, tribute, and sacrifice, divine about their participation in war (as "the many horse *qiang*"), agriculture, or the hunt (as the many *qiang*). The many *qiang* either referred to groups of *qiang* serving the king in analogy to "the many archers," or to handlers or officials in charge of them in analogy to "the many dogs" or "the many horses." If we favor the interpretation that they were barbarian mercenaries then they may have been analogous to the archers, if we favor the interpretation that they were slaves then the analogy to dogs and horses is a better fit. Given the massive use of *qiang* among other categories of captive in human sacrifice, the frequent inclusion of the rope grapheme around their necks and inscriptions about capturing escaped *qiang* as well as other lines of evidence (Campbell 2018), I favor the interpretation that *qiang* originally meant "slave" (lit. "those who are forced") and that its use as an ethnonym was an extension in keeping with Early Chinese "barbarian" naming practices using derogatory characters such as the later *Xiongnu* (lit. "fierce slaves").

In addition to inscription-based arguments for the existence of slaves, recent osteoarchaeological and isotopic work on sacrificial victims in the royal cemetery adds further lines of evidence. The bones of the sacrificial victims (Figure 9) showed pathologies indicative of years of malnourishment and ill-treatment (Wolin 2018), while isotopic analysis of their bones and teeth showed that their early life diets differed from those of Yinxu commoners as well as their own diets in the years before their deaths. Moreover, those diets were poor, patterning with Yinxu's pigs, dogs, and rats rather than its commoners (Cheung et al. 2017). These results strongly indicate that at least some of those sacrificed were held in captivity for years before their eventual deaths. These facts, together with the inscriptional evidence concerning various sorts of dependents and the frequent divinations about taking captives suggest that there was a population of slaves from which sacrificial victims were drawn. At the same time, and with the caveats that the royal divinations were only interested in a small subset of economic activities and that the king's agricultural divinations likely mostly concerned his own fields, the fact that *qiang* or other categories of captive appear agricultural divinations so rarely suggests that their economic role may have been minor in comparison to corvee labor.

5 Forms of Distribution and Commercialization

As mentioned earlier, the fundamental nature of the Shang economy is a matter of debate. While models of production and consumption play roles in that debate, the crux of the matter is exchange. For most of the English and Japanese language scholarship, markets, and money did not develop until the middle of the first millennium BCE. This scholarship has followed K. C. Chang's famous observation that the Shang civilization was built on political innovations with an economy unchanged from the Neolithic (Chang 1983). Exchange mechanisms in the Shang and Western Zhou are conceptualized as limited to tribute and gifting – essentially an elite redistribution model (Cook 1997; Liu and Chen 2003; Underhill and Fang 2004; Von Glahn 2016). Given the focus of Bronze Age archaeology on elite contexts and material culture and the limited perspective of the oracle-bone and bronze inscriptions, an elite-centric economic picture derived from those sources is unsurprising. The Chinese language scholarship has been more influenced by perspectives drawn from later texts and tends to take markets and trade for granted (Zhongguo 2003; Yang and Ma 2010). Recent scholarship, however, drawing on systematic archaeological analysis, explicit modeling, and holistic study of contemporaneous sources has advanced the debate and added new layers of complexity (Li 2019; Campbell 2021b; Campbell et al. 2022).

5.1 Prestige Goods

Beginning with prestige goods and high-value commodities there is abundant evidence for elite gifting – both inferiors "contributing" or "bringing" things to superiors and the king and other elites rewarding subordinates for services rendered (Campbell 2018). As mentioned earlier the king most commonly divines about the receipt of captives and cattle but horses, exotic animals, oracle-bones, and other things appear in the oracle-bone inscriptions as well. This practice is often interpreted as "tribute," but given the context of uncertainty implicit in divination, it is unclear how routinized these upward exchanges were. Jades were also gifted or given in "tribute" – as seen in the Huadong Prince's divinations (Schwartz 2013) and the jade blades from queen Fu Hao's tomb stating that they were "contributed" (Zhongguo 1980). Somewhat strangely – at least from the perspective of the elite-redistributive model – is the fact that nearly the only thing awarded by the king and other elites to subordinates in the longer bronze inscriptions that appear toward the end of the Late Shang are cowrie shells. The giving of the cowries occasions the casting of the bronze on which the inscription appears and some scholars read this to literally mean the bronze vessel was cast using the cowries as payment (Ma 1986). Whether or not this interpretation is accepted there is no other evidence concerning how elites acquired their bronze vessels and the traditional view is that cowries served as money, a topic that will be returned to in Section 5.3. Given that the giver of the cowries is not always the king, the reward of cowries cannot be seen as royal permission to have a bronze cast, and, as argued earlier, it is unlikely that the king exercised direct control over all of the bronze foundries at Yinxu in any case. The most likely scenario for the casting of ritual bronzes is instead some combination of sumptuary rules, possible alliances between lineages controlling production and those desiring bronzes cast, and payment. Thus, if many prestige goods were exchanged among elites in simple circuits of hierarchical elite gifting, more complex mechanisms existed as well, and even prestige goods acquisition was likely partially commercialized. Additional evidence of trade includes the derivation of things like stoneware (including proto-porcelain), nephrite, copper, lead, tin, and cowrie shells from beyond the reach of the Shang king's ability to project power (Campbell 2014; Campbell et al. 2022), as well as the appearance of traders in the oracle-bone inscriptions associated with horses, salt and spiced wine (Schwartz 2013; Cao 2014). Both horizontal and vertical exchange (trade and tribute) between elite lineages are implied by the lineage-based craft specialization, uneven distribution of resources, and the hierarchical nature of Shang society, but the actual mechanisms are not clear. To what degree exchanges were based on mutual benefit as opposed to force of arms or hierarchy and to what degree they were conducted by elites as opposed to traders or other delegates was likely variable and depended on factors like relative power, inter-group relations, distance, and type of good or service. In the hierarchical lineage model, each elite lineage functioned as a political-economic interest, with its own allegiances, alliances, subordinates, and agents acquiring prestige goods via gifting, tribute, and trade according to its status and means. If there were royal monopolies in either raw materials or finished goods – as many assert based on early state or later textual models (Liu and Chen 2003; Zhongguo 2003; Li 2019) – there is no direct evidence of it. Given the overall hegemonic lineage model of Shang political-economic organization (Keightley 1983; Campbell 2009; Campbell 2018; Lin 2019), it is more likely that Shang kings had privileged access to valuable resources and prestige goods through their position as lineage leader of lineage leaders, a strategic place atop the flows of gifting and tribute, and unmatched ability to project power.

5.2 Staple Goods

As argued earlier, the king and other elites appear to have their own estates on which they levied corvee labor and raised fighting forces. This sort of fiscal system, based primarily on labor rather than taxes in kind is also attested in the Inca (D'Altroy 2009; Campbell 2021b). From an exchange perspective, it implies that rural populations had their own fields as well as those they worked for their local lord. Thus, from the perspective of food, rural populations were likely mostly self-sufficient in grain, but would almost certainly have participated in lineage sacrificial and feasting events that served to redistribute meat and alcohol. These mechanisms were even more prominent in the capital where royal and other high elite rituals were hosted and sacrificial meat distributed in abundance. How dwellers of the Great Settlement Shang received other types of food is less clear. Elites likely provisioned themselves and their dependents from their estates, and it is possible that craftworkers received a grain stipend from their patrons, but it is also probable given the enormous size of the capital that some foodstuffs were acquired via formal exchange mechanisms and markets.

Given the evidence of craft specialization and the wide distribution of non-locally produced artifacts, the Shang economy was clearly far more integrated than prior scholarship claimed. The question is how? One recent model essentially extends the previous assumptions about royal control and redistribution and posits top-down mechanisms that would have to be extended even to quotidian goods and remote villages. A potential analogue would be the Inca (D'Altroy 2009), and it has the advantage of matching the evidence concerning Shang agriculture and redistributive feasting (Campbell 2021b, 2022). This model moreover claims that cowries did not serve as money and retains the primitivist perspective that markets did not emerge until the mid-first millennium and the appearance of metal coinage (Li 2003; Yang 2011; Von Glahn 2016; Li 2019).

The other model argues for the existence of formal exchange mechanisms, money, and markets in addition to elite gifting and some lineage redistributive institutions (Campbell et al. 2022). The first line of evidence is the sheer size of Yinxu, the complexity of its economy, and the lack of any evidence for the sort of redistributive infrastructure expected for a centralized economy. Additionally, there is the deep-time evidence of local product specialization and both elite and non-elite exchange extending back into the Neolithic. A third line of evidence is the development of the large-scale Yinxu workshops out of smaller and more generalized production models typical of earlier centers. This is especially true of bone-working where it has already been argued that the focus on high-value added artifacts was motivated by comparative advantage and profit. If polity-level provisioning was the goal of these workshops it is not clear why they specialized in and mass-produced only those artifacts for which their comparative advantages in raw materials, scale, and technology gave them the greatest return for the least effort and left the manufacture of less difficult or labor-intensive artifacts to small-scale bone crafters. The dispersed nature of these workshops argues against centralized control of their products while the distribution of those products across the Shang kingdom implies well-developed exchange mechanisms. Likewise, the evidence for widespread small-scale craft specialists for various non-elite goods on one end of the spectrum, and the presence of traders in the retinues of elites on the other, both suggest formal (impersonal) exchange mechanisms. Finally, there is the fact that even rural non-elites like those at Guandimiao participated in a wide range of nonoverlapping exchange networks, producing for local and regional exchange while consuming a range of goods such as shell and stone tools, bronze knives, and mass-produced hairpins, as well as cowrie shells, which derived from local or regional, inter-regional and long-distance exchange respectively. Rural villages were not self-sufficient and acquired even quotidian things like shell and stone tools from external sources, implying non-elite exchange mechanisms analogous to and probably developing from those of earlier times. Thus, while the institution of lineages and the lineage polity more generally had some redistributive functions – levying labor and distributing sacrificial meat – and gifting, tribute, and elite largesse were important aspects of the Shang economy – most craft products were likely exchanged via formal commercial exchange mechanisms.

5.3 Money

While cowry shells have long been considered currency in ancient China, this view has come into question recently in the English-language scholarship (Cook 1997; Li 2003; Von Glahn 2016). The argument proceeds from the primitivist assumptions of the elite-redistributive model. Because cowry shells are chiefly found in tombs or chariot team trappings their primary function is claimed to be ritual or ornamental. Western Zhou (ca. 1050–771 BCE) bronze inscriptions that other scholars have interpreted as evidence of the use of cowries as money are reinterpreted by this scholarship as merely recording gift exchanges between elites leading to the conclusion that cowries only began to serve as a measure of value (but not a medium of exchange) by the middle Western Zhou (Li 2003: 3). There are several issues with this argument. The first is source-bias. Given that the context of the early Western Zhou bronze inscriptions was largely to commemorate rewards given by the king and other high elites, the fact that commercial transactions are rare should not be taken as evidence that they did not happen. That cowry shells are mostly found in burials is not very significant given the fact that tomb contexts are virtually the only contexts where anything of value survives from the Shang. Moreover, Shang and Western Zhou elite-ritual contexts have been the nearly exclusive focus of textual scholars and archaeologists. To assume this represents the entire economy is problematic, especially in the face of evidence to the contrary. Even putting aside the tendentious primitivist readings of Western Zhou bronze inscriptions, the evolutionary assumption that the Shang economy was less commercialized than that of the Western Zhou because it was antecedent is unproven. Finally, the idea that ritual or decorative use excludes monetary function is not in keeping with current thinking on the anthropology of money (Haselgrove and Krmnicek 2012). In fact, this would exclude most forms of premodern money, including later Chinese metal coins which were also placed in burials analogously to cowries.

The positive evidence for the use of cowries as money rests on a number of lines of indirect evidence. As mentioned previously, cowries were nearly the only thing commemorated as an elite reward in the bronze inscriptions. At the same time, though cowries are principally found in tombs and sometimes in large quantities, they are not part of the core assemblage marking ritual status and are only weakly correlated with tomb size (Tang 2004; Campbell 2018). In addition, although cowries are nearly always pierced, are counted in strings in Shang inscriptions, and were sometimes found in tombs in strings, they only rarely occur in decorative contexts as parts of larger compositions – unlike jade, turquoise, tooth, shell, bronze, etc (Figure 11). Later Chinese coins were also kept on strings and the provisioning of the dead with food and money is a tradition that continues to this day (Figure 12). If elites received cowries but cowries were not crucial for Shang rituals nor major markers of mortuary status, nor prominent in ornamentation, then what were they for? Moreover, cowries were not limited to the elites but were ubiquitous in non-elite contexts as well, even in rural village sites like Guandimiao (Campbell et al. 2022).

The Shang Economy 45

Figure 11 Shang cowrie shells from Dasikong non-mortuary contexts with holes for string. (Zhongguo 2014, plate 30-1).

Figure 12 Chinese coins on strings (ancient currency gallery, Handan City Museum, CC 0 1.0).

Finally, all of the graphs concerning commerce in early Chinese scripts, including "trader/trade," "buy/sell," "treasure/valuable" include the graph for cowrie as a semantic component. If we take into account the above arguments that at least some aspects of elite and non-elite exchange occurred through formal mechanisms it stands to reason that there were at least commodities of exchange – easily quantifiable and exchangeable things that could serve as stores of value and units of account. Cowry shells are the most obvious candidate, but rolls of textile, bricks of salt, ingots of metal, livestock, etc. may have also served in some of these capacities, as indeed some of them did in later times.

5.4 Exchange

Specialization of economic function implies exchange. The previous section has described the various ways in which specialization existed within the Shang economy. The types of exchange depend on the types of goods or resources and the nature of the parties involved. Beginning with regime finance and the polity as a whole, as argued in section three, the evidence suggests a minimization of transportation costs – mobile or high-value things were extracted, while bulk commodities were consumed locally. This fits the evidence of the king and other elites as being highly mobile and suggests that commercial exchange likely fit similar patterns – bulk goods (fuel, grain, quotidian pottery, etc.) largely being exchanged in local circuits, while higher value or easier to transport things traveled larger distances. That even rural producers were involved in the exchange is demonstrated by the Erlitou period Huizui and the Late Shang Guandimiao sites – with even things like stone spades, ceramics, or pigs being produced for exchange, while in the latter case, cowries, hairpins, and a few metal objects show connections to larger exchange networks.

If elites exchanged gifts, tribute, and rewards with one another, guested and hosted, took booty from enemies, and taxed and levied subordinate labor, much of the Shang economy is difficult to account for in those terms. This is seen most clearly in the urban economy of the Great Settlement Shang and by shifting focus to consumption. The non-mortuary artifact assemblages recovered from loci outside the palace-temple area at Yinxu include shell, stone, bronze, bone, and ceramic artifacts as well as animal remains related to consumption and sometimes bone-working. To take the Dasikong excavation report (Zongguo 2014: 118) as an example, 1269 artifacts of ceramic, stone, bronze, antler, tooth, shell, and bone were recovered from residential contexts that ranged from elite to non-elite. Nearly half of this number were ceramics including cooking, serving, eating, and drinking vessels as well as ceramic net weights, spindle whorls, stamps, and other things. Ceramics are the most common form of material culture recovered from excavations at Yinxu but until recently kilns have rarely been found (Stoltman et al. 2009; Zhongguo 2012). Where did the population of the Great Settlement Shang get their pottery? The one production site that has been discovered at Yinxu suggests it was specialized in the production of fine-paste serving ware (Yinxu Work Team 2012). Combined with the evidence of specialized pottery production at Guandimiao, it suggests that ceramic production was not ubiquitous but concentrated in the hands of specialist producers and generally acquired through exchange. The few pieces of stoneware are the remains of prestige goods that were likely produced in the Yangzi region and imported via long-distance trade (Zhongguo 2003). The stone artifacts were mostly ground stone tools made of a variety of nonlocal stones and were likely produced (at least in blank form) at small sites close to quarries. As different types of tools use different sorts of stones, they represent multiple sources and diverse exchange networks. Forty small bronze artifacts were also found – mostly arrowheads, but also awls, a chisel, and two knives. These were almost certainly produced in one of the Yinxu bronze foundries, most likely the one located nearby and possibly associated with the residents. The bone, tooth, and antler artifacts are similar to assemblages found at other Yinxu loci – dominated by hairpins produced in the large-scale bone workshops, but also containing a diversity of weapons, tools, and ornaments ranging from formal to expedient. Many of these may have been acquired from the bone workshop associated with Dasikong. Three different types of cowries were recovered as well as small seashells with an inverse relationship between frequency and size. All of these represent inter-regional if not long-distance exchange and it is possible to see the twenty-nine shells recovered as different denominations of currency lost during the run of daily life. The thirty-one blades made of freshwater clam-shell are commonly found in Shang sites, and the clam may have been locally available in the Huan River, but the fact that they appear even in Guandimiao with no river nearby and the general model of Shang crafting suggests that they may well have been produced by communities of specialist crafters located near a rich source of the clams and then exchanged. As at other Shang sites, a large number of oracle-bone fragments were recovered, using turtle plastrons and carapaces, cattle scapula, and a few pelvises. Two scapulas were inscribed with calendrical notation, a rare occurrence outside the palace-temple area. The divinatory material raises the question of where residents of Dasikong acquired their turtles and cattle scapula and who was responsible for preparing and divining them. This, in turn, raises the issue of the Shang ritual economy.

All Shang communities, whether rural or urban, participated in divinatory, sacrificial, and mortuary rituals. In rural communities like Guandimiao, it is likely that at least the cattle bones used in divination are derived from local sacrifice and consumption events. The turtles may have been caught nearby, but the number of records of royal requests for and subordinate contributions of plastrons suggest that turtle plastrons were highly valued (Hou et al. 2018). In fact, compared to royal oracle-bones which utilized the best materials, the Dasikong and Guandimiao assemblages show an interesting distribution – relatively few turtle bones, a large majority of cattle scapula, and a few pelvises. This suggests that turtles were not monopolized by the court but were nonetheless valuable, cattle bones were relatively easy to come by and non-elites would sometimes make do with pelvises when no scapula were available. Given the urban location of the Dasikong residents, the turtles or carapaces and plastrons were necessarily acquired from elsewhere via some sort of exchange. While the cattle bones used for divination could have derived from cattle consumed in lineage sacrificial rites, those cattle and the other sacrificial livestock and slaves had to be acquired as well. While it is possible that elite lineages could have provisioned their sacrifices from their own estates and levies from subordinate populations, it is unlikely that every vocational lineage in the Great Settlement Shang had their own estates. Thus, the urban lineage ritual was likely supported by trade in animals and animal parts.

Probably the best evidence for non-elite and lesser elite consumption comes from burials. Although this fact is partially an artifact of preservation, it is nevertheless true that, as a society in which the dead occupied a privileged position (Keightley 2000), everything was at stake in the provisioning and ancestralization of the newly deceased (Puett 2004; Campbell 2016, 2018). As a result, the vast majority of the burial population at Yinxu were provisioned with at least a basic Shang mortuary assemblage. This included ceramic *gu* and *jue* drinking vessels, a cowry shell or two, a coffin, frequently a dog buried in a small pit below the coffin, other types of ceramic vessels, food offerings, and sometimes small articles of jade or bronze – often weapons (Tang 2004; Campbell 2018). Many of these mortuary objects were made especially for burial and would have had to have been obtained from specialists. Ceramic *gu* and *jue* were made for burial and became miniaturized over time, while the bronze artifacts in lesser elite tombs were increasingly thin or replaced copper and tin with lead. Specially made burnished pottery imitating bronzes are also known from late phase tombs (He 2006). Even the dog sacrifices were puppies or juvenile dogs, possibly indicating the specialized raising of young dogs for death ritual (Li and Campbell 2019). Considering the large population of the Great Settlement Shang, the demand for non-elite or lesser elite mortuary goods must have been considerable. As with goods of daily use discussed above, virtually none of the mortuary artifacts are likely to have been produced by those who used them. Ordinary urban lineage members, who had their own professions, would have needed to acquire some mortuary items from the bronze foundries, others from ceramic specialists, still others from carpenters, as well as possibly sacrificial puppies from those who raised them. The higher the rank and richer the tomb, the more craft specialists involved and the greater the investment of resources and need for exchange.

While it might be tempting to interpret the redundant industrial areas as self-sufficient alliances of crafting lineages with each cluster provisioning the lineages within it, that would be to ignore the prodigious size of the workshops and the evidence that they were producing for consumption beyond the local. The fact that the workshops of the capital were producing for exchange and that there was a widespread and large-scale demand for both the necessities of daily life and for mortuary ritual suggests a relation between the two. Either this exchange was managed at the lineage level or individuals acquired goods for themselves. While some degree of cooperation or coordination within larger kin groups is probable for collective endeavors like agriculture, lineage ritual, and war, the size of dwelling and consumption units suggests that for many things the most basic economic unit of Shang society was the nuclear family. Thus, while undoubtedly embedded in larger networks of kinship rights and obligations, much of the economic activity of Shang urban commoners was organized at the individual or family level. Bringing all of these lines together – the high degree of specialization and division of labor, the mass-producing workshops, the huge population and demand for diverse goods and services, and the small size of the basic economic unit all point to commercialization and formal exchange mechanisms in addition to informal and kin-based ones.

5.5 Markets and Trade

As mentioned earlier, the idea that there were no markets in China until the middle of the first millennium BCE has become the consensus view in the English-language literature despite being based on nothing more than primitivist assumptions and an absence of evidence. As with money, a closer look at the evidence makes this view increasingly untenable. The high degree of economic inter-dependency among both urban and rural commoners means that rather than an upper stratum of elites gifting prestige goods to one another while extracting tribute from an otherwise self-sufficient peasantry, there was either a redistributive economy more widespread and penetrating than anything even the Qin was able to create a millennium later, or, there was a significant degree of commercialization and formal mechanisms for exchange. The case for the later scenario has already been made, as has that for money – but what about actual markets? Later Chinese capitals and other major cities were also major commercial hubs often with multiple marketplaces (Von Glahn 2016). The work in the last couple of decades has overturned the idea that Yinxu was merely a ritual and mortuary center and demonstrated that it was also a center of population and industry (Zhongguo 2003; Tang 2009; Jing et al. 2013; Campbell 2014). In other words, it is now recognized that Shang Yinxu was a massive center of production and consumption, but somehow not of exchange. This is obviously untenable. Nevertheless, despite indirect evidence of money and commercialization in the Shang economy, no physical marketplaces have been identified. Based on later Chinese analogies, the leading candidates for marketplaces would be the industrial areas and, indeed, commerce may have provided the rationale for the clustering together of so many unrelated crafts. In the Han dynasty, for instance, workshops were often located in or near the marketplaces (Barbieri-Low 2007).

6 Economic Change Over Time

6.1 Pre-Shang

In the case of Chinese archaeology, long-term economic development can best be seen in terms of changes in urbanism, craft production, and exchange. As mentioned in Section 1, China saw the rise and development of multiple regional polities with large centers in the third millennium BCE. Though the study of most of these sites is still in its infancy, they appear to be diverse in organization (Shelach and Jaffe 2014; Campbell et al. 2022). Nevertheless, they all show evidence of long-distance exchange in prestige goods as well as regional and local exchange of raw materials and finished goods (Shelach-Lavi 2015; Campbell et al. 2022). The Erlitou center can be seen as a point of transition in the eighteenth century BCE – at 300 ha it was similar in size to the preceding centers of the third millennium but it was also the first major site of the Central Plains Bronze Age and direct ancestor to Yinxu (Campbell 2014). It had the first major bronze casting foundries, and these as well as turquoise and bone workshops are all associated with or in the vicinity of the palace-temple precinct. At the same time, the bronze foundry remains are modest compared to those of Zhengzhou or Yinxu while the bone workshops appear small-scale and produced a wide range of artifacts (Campbell et al. 2022). Thus, on the one hand, there seems to be early evidence of a relationship between certain forms of prestige good crafting and elites, and, on the other, a generalist model of production for at least some of these industries. At the same time, sourcing studies and work at the site of Nanwa have shown that white ceramics, an Erlitou period prestige good, were produced in and sourced from a number of places (Liu, Chen, and Li 2007; Zhengzhou daxue 2014). At the other end of the spectrum, the site of Huizhui specialized in the production of spades from local stone sources and exchanged them widely (Ford 2008). In other words, in addition to some crafting that may have been attached to the palace-temples or at least focused on provisioning the ruling elites and their retinues, there is also evidence of prestige and non-prestige goods being manufactured for exchange.

There is, unfortunately, no evidence concerning staple finance – whether taxation was in kind or in labor – nor have any granaries been identified. From a ritual economy perspective, however, the Erlitou site is clearly ancestral to developments that come to full fruition at Yinxu. Erlitou has both animal and human sacrificial deposits, rich elite tombs and assemblages of jade blades as well as feasting and drinking vessels that include the first ritual bronzes. At the same time, however, compared to Yinxu, the sacrificial deposits are meager, the tombs are small and relatively poor, and the ritual sets are composed of a mixture of small ceramic, lacquer, and bronze vessels. While the difference in the ritual economies at the Erlitou and Yinxu sites is undoubtedly partially due to 500 years of developments in technology and crafting efficiency and the fact that the center of Yinxu was ten times the size of Erlitou, there are other differences as well. The mortuary ritual at Erlitou was not only less hierarchical than at Yinxu, it was also less inclusive – the majority of the burial population were interred without coffins or grave goods (Campbell 2018). This obviously has ramifications for the mortuary economy – it is not clear that the Erlitou period had crafting specifically dedicated to the dead as opposed to elite-ritual sets that could be included in mortuary assemblages. Moreover, evidence of human sacrifice is rare and bovids, especially cattle, are far less common than at Yinxu. The former fact indicates that there was much less sacrificial expenditure of potentially useful human labor, while the latter is significant because sheep and cattle have far greater potential for being driven long distances and thus greatly expand the catchment for sacrificial feasting resources. All this is to say that despite the fact that all the major elements of the Yinxu ancestral ritual economy are there in embryonic stage at the Erlitou site – mortuary ritual, sacrifice, and feasting – they occur at a much smaller scale and were possibly less hierarchical in nature (Campbell 2018).

6.2 The Early Shang Period

For the Early Shang period, both the fact that the contemporary city of Zhengzhou sits atop the Shang center and a relative lack of studies focused on economy mean that many things remain unclear. While there is no evidence of palace-temple-associated prestige goods or other dedicated provisioning, there are clear developments in craft production with more and larger ritual bronzes cast, multiple foundries, and a variety of workshops located in the Zhengzhou center. There is, moreover, scattered evidence of small-scale and expedient crafting at various Early Shang sites. This suggests that, generally speaking, small to medium-scale generalist production existed – provisioning elite and non-elite patrons – as well as a certain amount of expedient or nonspecialist craft depending on the industry. Some workshops, such as lapidary and high-skill bone and woodwork may have been associated with the rulers, as at Yinxu and possibly Erlitou, but there is no direct evidence. The expansion of the bronze industry in Early Shang times, however, may have provided the initial model of large-scale workshops more generally.

The ritual economy likewise develops from Erlitou times. Mortuary investment as well as sacrifice increased, but the relative quantity and sacrificial role of cattle and sheep is much the same as it was at Erlitou. If there was redistributive feasting it was largely based on pigs and thus local provisioning networks. The number and type of ritual bronzes increased dramatically in this period and, for elites, these vessels replaced ceramic and lacquer vessels in ritual sets. The need to provision elites with bronze ritual vessels made the Zhengzhou foundries the central nodes of expansive networks of exchange, production, and consumption.

6.3 The Middle Shang Period

While the Middle Shang period is less well-understood and possibly a time of political decentralization, economic development nevertheless continued. This fact alone suggests that previous models emphasizing Early Chinese economic centralization and control are incorrect. Bronze foundries and bone workshops have been discovered within the Huanbei walled center just north of Yinxu. Preliminary research on the bone workshop suggests fine, high labor investment crafting typical of elite provisioning. Analysis of bone-working of this period at the regional center of Daxinzhuang shows small-scale, generalist bone-working, suggesting that the major types of production seen for the Early Shang period are all present during this period as well.

Although large-scale burial comparanda are relatively rare for this period, a study of mortuary development showed that tomb hierarchy continued to elaborate even while death rituals became more inclusive (Campbell 2018). Both human and cattle sacrifice increased in this period (Huang 2004; Yuan and Flad 2005; Campbell 2018) and it is possible that redistributive feasting became more important. Bronze vessels became larger and vessel types more elaborate, showing that investment in ritual during this period continued to expand. Moreover, the evidence of the increasing spread of bronze-casting technology and the proliferation of foundries during this period (Bagley 1999) points to a widespread elite demand for ritual goods and a lack of centralized exchange mechanisms.

6.4 The Late Shang Period

In terms of craft production, the Late Shang can be divided in two. In the first two phases of the site, the workshops of the Great Settlement began relatively modest in scale and at first continued the patterns of earlier Central Plains centers with workshops associated with the palace-temple area producing mostly prestige goods, workshops located elsewhere producing a range of things, but what would become the large-scale bone workshops already beginning to specialize in hairpin production.

At the same time, the reign of Yinxu's first king, Wu Ding, inaugurated a number of dramatic changes in the ritual economy. Oracle-bone divination, a long-practiced form of osteomancy, became stratified and its most developed form, involving sawing, drilling, chiseling, and inscribing, became associated with the royal court. Human sacrifice was practiced on a scale never seen before or since in Eurasian history, while cattle, sheep, and other livestock were brought from near and far for rituals of unprecedented magnitude. The largest Shang bronze ever cast dates from this period (the 875 kg Si Mu Wu Ding) as does the unlooted tomb of queen Fu Hao – the richest burial known from the Shang. For the first time, Shang kings were buried in great four-ramped tombs oriented to the four quarters and orders of magnitude larger than any previous East Asian burial. At the same time as it reached unprecedented levels of stratification, the Shang mortuary ritual became more inclusive as well, with the vast majority of the burial population equipped with at least basic tomb furnishings (Tang 2004; Campbell 2018).

Beginning approximately halfway through the Late Shang a number of changes took place, possibly related to military setbacks in the north-west. Regardless of the underlying reason, the Shang kingdom seems to undergo structural reforms tending toward greater systematization of political and ritual organization (Keightley 1983; Jiang 2012; Campbell 2018). At the same time, the Great Settlement Shang grew to its maximum size even as the bone and bronze workshops increased in scale. Whatever territorial setbacks may have befallen the kingdom at large, the capital itself prospered as never before.

In terms of the ritual economy, human sacrifice appears to be scaled back, increasingly replaced by cattle specially raised for the purpose (Hu 1974; Campbell 2018). The consumption of beef overtook pork in this period, even among non-elites (Li 2009; Cheung et al. 2017), possibly indicating the growing importance of redistributive feasting. This period saw the organization of royal ritual into a system of daily rites providing both a system for elite time reckoning and a continuous round of rituals. Though apparently smaller in scale than some of the great ceremonies of Wu Ding's time, the cost of daily royal sacrifice could not have been small. In the realm of mortuary ritual, an analogous systematization and economization seems to have occurred. Though tombs became larger and status was increasingly stratified, it was often more in terms of symbolic than economic capital (Jiang 2012). Miniaturized ceramic drinking vessels, burnished bronze-imitating ceramics, and lead and thin-walled bronze vessels become more and more prevalent in late-period tombs (He 2006). This suggests both that fewer and fewer actual ritual assemblages were being sequestered with the dead and that the specialized production of mortuary objects had become a major component of craft production. Rather than signaling a decline in the ritual economy, these developments at Yinxu during the second half of the Late Shang period should be seen as a diversification of ritual possibly entailing even greater economic expenditures. Indeed, the expansion of the bronze foundries during Yinxu's last phases suggests as much.

In sum, Shang Yinxu at its peak saw not only an increase in size from earlier Zhengzhou, but also several important economic developments. These included an increase in the number of workshops as well as the scale, and in some cases, specialization of their production. Wu Ding's innovations and the subsequent late-phase reforms expanded the economy of sacrifice, divination, and burial to a degree unseen in previous Central Plains Bronze Age centers. In addition to a huge increase in elite expenditures, these developments included the large-scale redistributive consumption of cattle, increasing non-elite participation in the ritual economy as consumers of specially produced mortuary goods and widespread, if stratified, divination. To reformulate K.C. Chang's observation about the basis of the Shang polity, Shang kingship, at Yinxu in particular, was based on political and ritual innovations, but these had large ramifications for economic development. As has been argued above, the expansion of the workshops and widespread demand for their products (ritual or otherwise) led to the increasing commercialization of exchange and served the elite lineages that controlled the production as a source of wealth. In the countryside, non-elite exchange in utilitarian goods continued as it had from Neolithic times, though it was increasingly integrated into larger systems of exchange.

6.5 Post-Shang Developments

Despite the Zhou conquest of the Shang, the general economic trends described above continued unabated, again suggesting a certain degree of independence of economic and political processes in Early China, or at least their lack of political centralization. While it has been argued that the Western Zhou polity differed from that of the Shang in having multiple simultaneous capitals, this difference may be more apparent than real. As noted above, the Shang kings traveled between estates, some of which may have been significant settlements, now buried beneath millennia of Yellow River flood alluvium. At the same time, the Zhouyuan, was a sprawling metropolitan center of elite lineages, workshops, and palaces, estimated to be over 30 km^2 in extent by the end of the Western Zhou – much like Yinxu. The organization of the workshops also replicated and developed upon the large-scale production facilities at Yinxu, strongly suggesting (along with other lines of evidence) that the craftspeople of the Shang capital were moved wholesale to the Zhouyuan upon the Zhou conquest. Multiple bronze casting foundries (Zhouyuan 2011), at least one large-scale bone workshop (Zhao 2017) and a workshop for the mass production of stone earrings, were all present in the Zhouyuan (Sun 2008). While the bronze workshop likely served local elite needs, the products of the bone workshop were more widely distributed and the stone earrings were not consumed locally at all (Sun 2008).

At the same time, in addition to the evidence of new types of manufacturing serving the needs of the large population of the Zhouyuan's elite and non-elite consumers, specialized workshop production spread beyond the Zhouyuan. In addition to workshops at other royal centers of the Wei River valley (Ye and Yu 1985), there is highly standardized and specialized bone-working at elite non-royal centers such as Guo (Ma, Wei, and Hou 2015), where one pit produced nearly two thousand pieces of neatly sawed debitage, blanks and finished artifacts of a single type of pin. Bronze foundries have also been discovered outside beyond the royal centers as well (Thote 2014), indicating that new technologies and modes of crafting did not remain concentrated in the royal centers for long.

The long-term significance of the rise and spread of large-scale and often highly specialized workshops is two-fold. The first is that, especially for the production of non-prestige goods, the existence and expansion of such workshops indicate increasing levels of commercialization and the importance of craft production as a source of revenue for at least some elites. And while we do not possess good information on rural non-elites in the Western Zhou period, given the expansion of non-prestige good production, it seems unlikely they were less tied into larger economic networks than their ancestors. The second significance is that the large-scale workshop model was a decisive factor in the production of cast iron beginning in the eighth century BCE (Lam 2014; Qian and Huang 2021). Cast iron is significant because although it lacks the tensile strength of hammered iron, it can be produced at scale, a feature that led to its mass production during the Industrial Revolution. The reason why cast iron was not adopted in Europe and the Near East until roughly two thousand years after China was that cast iron requires high-temperature furnaces and mass production. The former is a technical requirement as iron melts at over 1500 degrees

Celsius, while the latter is an economic necessity as hammered iron is a superior though more labor-intensive material. The advanced bronze casting technology and the large-scale workshop model of the Shang and their further development in the Western Zhou bequeathed both requirements to the first iron foundries. Cast iron, moreover, had economic ramifications far beyond those of cast bronze. Because iron is a much more abundant ore than copper or tin, it has greater potential for large-scale production and utilitarian use. With the advent of mass-produced cast-iron tools of production, agriculture, and craft were transformed and the economy with it. It may be that cast iron and not the advent of markets, as some older scholarship would have it, lay behind the dramatic demographic and economic changes seen in the Eastern Zhou. In fact, the difference between Western and Eastern Zhou agriculture was not crops. The millet-wheat-legume basis of north Chinese multi-cropping was already well-established by the early centuries of the first millennium BCE (Lee et al. 2007; Yuan et al. 2020). It was more likely the introduction and widespread use of iron spades and axes for digging wells and felling trees that opened up the land to demographic expansion even as iron plows made agriculture more productive.

The ritual economy continued to be an important aspect of both polity-level and personal expenditures, with the tombs of rulers becoming ever larger, culminating in the famous mausoleum of the first emperor at the end of the third century BCE. At the same time, as lineage ritual decreased in broad-based political importance, there was increasing scope for individual mortuary expression for those who could afford it. In fact, the resources that some were spending on funerals prompted philosophers to present arguments for frugal burial. Beyond funerals, state rituals could also become significant economic burdens with some Han emperors having to reduce the number of sacrifices and shrines in times of financial strain. Though thoroughly transformed over intervening millennia, the legacy of the Shang ritual economy in terms of funerary and lineage rituals remained important parts of state and personal economies down to relatively recent times.

Finally, the legacy of centuries of elite and non-elite exchange and increasing commercialization was the establishment of official markets and attempts by the king to regulate and tax trade. One remarkable bronze inscription dating to the ninth century BCE records a Zhou king rewarding an aristocrat for military service by putting him in charge of regulating and taxing the "accumulated goods" of the four quarters and the Eastern capital and economic hub of Chengzhou. Significantly this remit included both regulating tribute from a non-Zhou people but also other forms of exchange, including trade.

> They shall not dare to refuse to send out their silk, their accumulated goods (tribute?), their proffered people (hostages? servants?) or their commercial

goods. They shall not dare to refuse to approach the military outposts and the markets [with these things]. ... If they be our Many Lords and Hundred Surnames their trade goods must reach the markets. They shall not dare, moreover, to remit faulty or stolen goods for trade.
(translation based on Cook and Goldin 2016: 186).

Here we can see not only the management of tribute but also of trade through markets and outposts. Furthermore, the mention of both Zhou elites and commoners shows that both groups were engaged in commercial activity – in line with the archaeological evidence we have been assembling for the entire Bronze Age, if not earlier. The regulatory concern of the king in this case seems to be that trade took place only in official markets where it could be taxed and regulated, just as in official markets in later times. This had the dual benefit of being a source of polity revenue and, at the same time, providing assurance to consumers that the goods they purchased were neither flawed nor stolen.

Thus, despite the image of Bronze Age elites as preoccupied only with war, ritual, and hunting derived from both contemporaneous inscriptional and later textual sources, they were also involved in commercial activity, and as the rise and proliferation of large-scale specialized crafting indicates, some likely drew considerable income from these activities. If this is so, then it appears that rather than presiding over an elite-redistributive economy, the role of at least some polity institutions was to regulate and tax market activity in a multifaceted and significantly commercialized economy. Rather than having to wait for the decline of the Zhou kingship and the social and political changes of the Eastern Zhou period, it was rather underlying and deep-time Bronze Age economic changes that paved the way for Eastern Zhou demographic and economic growth. Among the Bronze Age economic developments detailed in previous sections, the rise and spread of large-scale workshops was especially significant. Both sign of and impetus for increasing commercialization, crafting lineages leveraged technological, locational, and scalar advantages to reap unprecedented profits from their endeavors. This, in turn, fueled further innovation and the spread of large-scale workshops across the landscape and to new industries proliferated commercial goods and increased economic integration between urban and rural populations. The advent of mass-produced cast iron artifacts with its ramifications for Chinese demographic and economic growth could not have occurred without this development. In the end, it may be that K.C. Chang was both right and wrong. The Chinese Bronze Age *was* unique in the focus of its bronze industry on the casting of ritual vessels but rather than relegating the Early Chinese economy to stagnation until the mid-first millennium BCE, the bronze foundries were the model of a production format that was to have a transformative impact on the shape and direction of the Early Chinese economy.

7 Future Directions

Given that ancient economy is a relatively recent area of interest in Chinese archaeology it is not surprising that there are many areas of research that could be strengthened. These range from the theoretical to the empirical and from the application of explicit models and comparative frameworks to further integration of scientific techniques into holistic analyses.

In particular, the major features of the Shang economy outlined above all require further work. These are the concentration and growth of certain industries in the capital; the importance of lineages to an economic organization; the provisioning of the urban mega-centers that characterized the Chinese Bronze Age; the economic role of small, rural sites; the nature and degree of commercialization and trade; the organization of political finance around mobility – taxation in terms of labor and livestock, flows of mobile resources to the center and movement of the court across the land.

7.1 Craft Production

While craft production studies have been on the rise in Chinese archaeology in the last two decades, there is still much work to be done. Unsurprisingly, bronze working has seen the lion's share of research, but bone-working studies have become more common and ceramic and stone tool production studies are also increasing. In addition to finding ways of studying more poorly preserved crafts such as woodworking and textiles, better preserving but poorly investigated crafts such as shell crafting, need attention as well. Further work on locating and studying resource acquisition sites and sourcing more generally is needed – understanding the contexts of resource acquisition and the networks of exchange they were enmeshed in would greatly enrich the study of the Shang economy.

In addition to filling in the holes regionally and chronologically for the various crafts mentioned, understanding them within larger economic models is crucial as well. Beyond *chaîne opératoire*, future work must investigate the ramifications of production case studies for exchange systems and consumption patterns. In addition, if bone-working had multiple modes and shows stratification according to products in the Late Shang, what of other crafts? Is there analogous product specialization in other industries and if so, what is its developmental history and ramifications for the economy in general? In addition, if, as I have argued, the advent of large-scale workshops was of particular significance for Early Chinese economic development, then more work on its manifestations prior to Yinxu and later spread is of crucial importance. What explains this form of organization and whose control was it under? This leads to questions of political-economic models more generally and refining ways of distinguishing between competing hypotheses.

7.2 Domestic Economy and Kinship

Many of the fundamentals of Shang economic life are all but unknown. Fine-grained research on well-preserved domestic contexts would go a long way to filling the huge gap in our knowledge concerning the daily life of most of the Shang population. Sampling with approaches such as micro-morphology, soil chemical analyses as well as screening and flotation, and, especially, their integration into larger, holistic analyses would yield a better understanding of Shang sites. In general, more systematic excavations of non-elite residential areas in urban and rural contexts would expand our knowledge of the Shang domestic economy. Osteobiography and osteometric analyses in general are of great significance for understanding individual lives as well as social dynamics of relevance to domestic economies. More as well as more fine-grained zooarchaeological and paleobotanical studies would also be of great assistance. These should include more studies of butchery, food processing, and cooking (Zhang 2022) as well as isotopic analyses (Cheung et al. 2017).

Much of the debate concerning the Shang economy revolves around different understandings of its wider social and political structures, especially the role of the lineage. What was the economic role of the lineage? Were commoners integrated into lineages or just elites? To what degree was cohabitation and profession structured by kinship? What is the history of lineages as institutions? Did Shang and Zhou lineages play the same economic roles? None of these questions have good answers and all of them are of crucial importance for modeling Chinese Bronze Age economies. Future genetic studies of lineage cemeteries would help with understanding the relatedness of those buried there, while more osteometric and isotopic analysis would be useful in exploring life histories, social roles, and inequality.

7.3 Agricultural Economy, Urban Provisioning, Environmental Impact

In general, how people acquired the basic essentials of daily life from food to fuel to housing is poorly understood for the entire Chinese Bronze Age. Further work in zooarchaeology at different types of sites and loci of large sites would clarify or complicate some of the preliminary patterns identified in the literature. Additional work on secondary products and husbandry practices would also help us to better understand how significant different secondary products were for the economy as well as how various taxa were being raised and where.

There is an even greater need for palaeobotanical studies at Yinxu and other Shang sites. Beyond basic research like crop ratios, understanding agricultural practices including plowing, hoeing, manuring, multi-cropping, and field rotation, the role of animal grazing, foddering, and providing dung as well as potential green manuring practices are all needed to better understand Shang agriculture in itself and in a developmental context. Work on irrigation and water management systems in general would provide further potential insights into agricultural systems and land use patterns. Systematic investigation of crop processing and grain storage facilities and practices could also potentially shine an important light on the Shang agricultural economy. Studies of fuels for cooking as well as for metallurgy and ceramics are needed. Were there woodcutters and charcoal makers in the Shang? If so, how much of the fuel consumed at the Great Settlement Shang was wood or charcoal as opposed to grass or dung? Where did Yinxu get all of its fuel and what was the impact on the local environment?

While much attention has been focused on moments of transition and their potential correlation with rapid climate change events like the 4.2–4.0 k BP event, less attention has been given to the climate during periods of development, or the impact of large-scale or long-term settlement on local environment. K.C. Chang once suggested that the historical record of Shang dynasty capital movements might have had to do with resource procurement (Chang 1980), but with the size of Chinese Bronze Age capital sites, it was more likely a push than a pull factor as local environments were exhausted and degraded. The human-environmental dynamics of Shang settlement are an important but underexplored part of the economic picture.

7.4 Small Sites and Rural Contexts

The rural site of Guandimiao is proving to be of great importance in overthrowing previous assumptions about the Shang economy, but it is just one example. It is impossible to know how typical Guandimiao is of Shang villages without more examples and it is likely that there was regional variation. Understanding how rural and urban, elite and non-elite economies were integrated will require a concerted effort to systematically explore small sites in different regions. Especially relevant issues are the degree of economic integration, the prevalence of crafting or resource extraction for exchange as well as the political–economic relationship with local elites. At Guandimiao itself the questions of how ceramic production was organized, the nature of its products, and what sort of exchange it participated in are crucial and will reveal much with potentially wide-ranging ramifications.

The significance of Guandimiao for the Shang economy, however, will always be limited by the fact that it is a single example.

7.5 Exchange, Commodities, and Money

With the traditional consensus that cowries served as money before metal coinage and the relatively new Western and Japanese view that Chinese Bronze Age economies were redistributive and lacked money, it is perhaps unsurprising that the debate has not moved beyond the presence/absence of money. Seeing money as an institution that reduces transaction costs – as something that can be a store of value, unit of account, and medium of exchange – also suggests a history of the institution and that potentially multiple things might have served these roles. What are the things that might have served these functions and what evidence do we have? Can the use of cowrie shells be quantified over time as a proxy for monetization? If elites and non-elites alike were engaged in exchange activities as we have demonstrated, how was this accomplished? Future research will have to untangle these questions with concerted efforts to understand Shang exchange systems holistically, including their institutions and relationships to different aspects of the economy. This, in turn, will require models, comparisons, and hypothesis testing.

7.6 Theoretical Models, Comparison, and the Significance of the Shang Economy

Work explicitly engaging various approaches to the study of the ancient economy would help identify new questions and generate novel results (Liu and Chen 2003; Campbell 2021b; Campbell et al. 2022). By making explicit assumptions and connecting results to an overarching model this sort of approach has the advantage of making clear the relationships between results and conclusions and linking specific findings to their larger significance. Thus, even if the models themselves prove faulty or new information overturns old conclusions, by making its assumptions explicit, this approach allows models to be easily improved and new conclusions generated. A more widespread adaptation of this sort of approach would help drive research on the Chinese Bronze Age economy forward.

A related issue is that of comparison. Despite progress in this direction over the last few decades, Chinese archaeology could increase its engagement with work in other areas in the world. Thus, further comparative work is desirable as well as the potential adoption of models and methods from other places. This will no doubt methodologically enrich the study of the Shang economy as well as raise new issues. Polity finance, for instance, is much better studied in a variety of ancient economic settings but has scarcely been broached as a serious research topic in Shang archaeology. With the wealth of archaeological information, depth of historical texts, and pace of work happening in China, Chinese archaeology and history surely have much to offer the world on the subject of comparative ancient economy.

References

Anyang Work Team, Institute of Archaeology, CASS. 2004. "Survey and Test Excavation of the Huanbei Shang City in Anyang." *Chinese Archaeology* 4 (1): 1–20. https://doi.org/10.1515/CHAR.2004.4.1.1.

———. 2018. "Henan Anyangshi Yinxu Liujiazhuang Beidi Qianding Zhucangkeng Fajue Baogao." *Kaogu*, (10): 32–41.

Bagley, Robert. 1999. "Shang Archaeology." In *The Cambridge History of Ancient China: From the Origins of Civilization to 221 BC*, edited by Michael Loewe and Edward L. Shaughnessy, 1st ed., 124–231. Cambridge: Cambridge University Press. https://doi.org/10.1017/CHOL9780521470308.

Barbieri-Low, Anthony J. 2007. *Artisans in Early Imperial China*. Seattle: University of Washington Press. www.jstor.org/stable/j.ctv21r3pn7.

Brunson, Katherine, Ren Lele, Zhao Xin, et al. 2020. "Zooarchaeology, Ancient mtDNA, and Radiocarbon Dating Provide New Evidence for the Emergence of Domestic Cattle and Caprines in the Tao River Valley of Gansu Province, Northwest China." *Journal of Archaeological Science: Reports* 31 (June): 102262. https://doi.org/10.1016/j.jasrep.2020.102262.

Campbell, Roderick. 2009. "Toward a Networks and Boundaries Approach to Early Complex Polities." *Current Anthropology* 50 (6): 821–48. https://doi.org/10.1086/648398.

———. 2012. "On Sacrifice: An Archaeology of Shang Sacrifice." In *Sacred Killing*, edited by Anne Porter, and Glenn M. Schwarz, 305–24. University Park: Penn State University Press. https://doi.org/10.1515/9781575066769-014.

———. 2013. "A Preliminary Inquiry into the Scale of Bronze Production at Anyang." In *Kaoguxue Shiye Xia de Chengshi, Gongyi Chuantong Yu Zhongwai Jiaoliu – Liu Qingzhu Xiansheng Qishi Huadan Qingshou Wenji*. Beijing: Science Press.

———. 2014. *Archaeology of the Chinese Bronze Age: From Erlitou to Anyang*. Los Angeles: Cotsen Institute of Archaeology Press. https://doi.org/10.2307/j.ctvdjrr9r.

———. 2016. "Memory, Power and Death in Chinese History and Prehistory." In *The Archaeology of Ancestors: Death, Memory, and Veneration*, edited by Erica Hill, and Jon B. Hageman, 81–101. Gainesville: University Press of Florida. https://doi.org/10.2307/j.ctvx076wp.

2018. *Violence, Kinship and the Early Chinese State: The Shang and Their World*. New York: Cambridge University Press.

2021a. "On Borders as an Archaeological/Historical Problem." In *Borders in Archaeology: Anatolia and the South Caucasus ca. 3500–500 BCE*, edited by Lorenzo d'Alfonso, and Karen Rubinson, 37–50. Ancient Near Eastern Studies 58. Leuven: Peeters.

2021b. "Taxing Questions: Financing the Chinese Bronze Age." In *Ancient Taxation: The Mechanics of Extraction in Comparative Perpective*, edited by Jonathan Valk, and Irene Soto Marín, 39–70. Isaw Monographs. New York: New York University Press.

2022. "Feeding the Great Settlement: Preliminary Notes on the Shang Animal Economy." In *Food Provisioning in Complex Societies: Zooarchaeological Perspectives*, edited by Levent Atici, and Benjamin S. Arbuckle, 92–107. Denver: University Press of Colorado.

Campbell, Roderick, Yitzchak Jaffe, Christopher Kim, Camilla Sturm, and Li Jaang. 2022. "Chinese Bronze Age Political Economies: A Complex Polity Provisioning Approach." *Journal of Archaeological Research* 30 (1): 69–116. https://doi.org/10.1007/s10814-021-09158-0.

Campbell, Roderick, Zhipeng Li, Yuling He, and Yuan Jing. 2011. "Consumption, Exchange and Production at the Great Settlement Shang: Bone-Working at Tiesanlu, Anyang." *Antiquity* 85 (330): 1279–97. https://doi.org/10.1017/S0003598X00062050.

Cao, Dazhi. 2014. "The Loess Highland in a Trading Network (1300–1050 BC)." Princeton: Princeton University. https://dataspace.princeton.edu/handle/88435/dsp01n583xv130.

2018. "Zuhui Neihan Yu Shangdai de Guojia Jiegou." *Gudai Wenming* 12: 71–122.

Chang, Kwang-chih. 1980. *Shang Civilization*. New Haven: Yale University Press.

1983. *Art, Myth, and Ritual: The Path to Political Authority in Ancient China*. Cambridge: Harvard University Press.

1986. *The Archaeology of Ancient China*, 4th ed. New Haven: Yale University Press.

Chen, Guoliang. 2021. Qun jiao cang cheng: Yanshi Shangcheng di XIII hao jianzhu jizhiqun chutan (Walled granary district: Preliminary investigation of the Yanshi Shangcheng number 8 architectural foundation group. http://kaogu.cssn.cn/zwb/xsyj/yjxl/jlycskg/202102/t20210223_5313227.shtml

Cheung, Christina, Zhichun Jing, Jigen Tang, and Michael P. Richards. 2017. "Social Dynamics in Early Bronze Age China: A Multi-Isotope Approach." *Journal of Archaeological Science: Reports* 16 (December): 90–101. https://doi.org/10.1016/j.jasrep.2017.09.022.

Cook, Constance A. 1997. "Wealth and the Western Zhou." *Bulletin of the School of Oriental and African Studies, University of London* 60 (2): 253–94.

Cook, Constance A., and Paul Rakita Goldin, eds. 2016. *A Source Book of Ancient Chinese Bronze Inscriptions*. Early China Special Monograph Series, No. 7. Berkeley, California: The Society for the Study of Early China.

Costin, Cathy. 1991. "Craft Specialization: Issues in Defining, Documenting, and Explaining the Organization of Production." *Archaeological Method and Theory* 3: 1–56.

Crabtree, Pam J. 2018. *Early Medieval Britain: The Rebirth of Towns in the Post-Roman West*. Case Studies in Early Societies. Cambridge: Cambridge University Press.

D'Altroy, Terence N. 2009. *The Incas*. The Peoples of America. Malden: Blackwell.

Falkenhausen, Lothar Von. 1993. "On the Historiographical Orientation of Chinese Archaeology." *Antiquity* 67 (257): 839–49. https://doi.org/10.1017/S0003598X00063821.

Fiskesjö, Magnus. 2001. "Rising from Blood-Stained Fields: Royal Hunting and State Formation in Shang China." *Bulletin of the Museum of Far Eastern Antiquities* 73: 48–192.

Flad, Rowan. 2018. "Urbanism as Technology in Early China." *Archaeological Research in Asia* 14 (June): 121–34. https://doi.org/10.1016/j.ara.2016.09.001.

Flad, Rowan K. 2008. "Divination and Power." *Current Anthropology* 49 (3): 403–37. https://doi.org/10.1086/588495.

Ford, Anne. 2008. "Ground Stone Tool Production at Huizui, China: An Analysis of a Manufacturing Site in the Yilou River Basin." *Bulletin of the Indo-Pacific Prehistory Association* 24: 71–78. https://doi.org/10.7152/bippa.v24i0.11872.

Fowles, Severin M. 2013. *An Archaeology of Doings: Secularism and the Study of Pueblo Religion*, 1st ed. Santa Fe, NM: School for Advanced Research Press.

Haselgrove, Colin, and Stefan Krmnicek. 2012. "The Archaeology of Money." *Annual Review of Anthropology* 41 (1): 235–50. https://doi.org/10.1146/annurev-anthro-092611-145716.

He, Yuling. 2006. "Yinxu Muzang Suizangpin Mingqihua Xianxiang Fenxi." *Sandai Kaogu* 2: 375–82.

2017. "Henan Anyang Huanbei Shangcheng zhutong, zhigu zuofang yizhi." *Dazhong Kaogu* 2017(1): 14–15.

Henansheng wenwu kaogu yanjiusuo. 2001. *Zhengzhou Shangcheng*. Beijing: Wenwu chubanshe.

Hou, Yanfeng, Roderick Campbell, Li Zhipeng, et al. 2018. "The Guandimiao Bone Assemblage (and What It Says about the Shang Economy)." *Asian Perspectives* 57 (2): 281–310.

Hou, Yanfeng, Roderick Campbell, Yan Zhang, and Suting Li. 2019. "Animal Use in a Shang Village: The Guandimiao Zooarchaeological Assemblage." *International Journal of Osteoarchaeology* 29 (2): 335–45. https://doi.org/10.1002/oa.2745.

Hu, Houxuan. 1974. "Zhongguo Nukang Shehui de Rexun He Renji." *Wenwu* (8): 56–68.

Huang, Zhanyue. 2004. *Gu dai ren sheng ren xun tong lun*. Beijing: Wenwu chubanshe.

Inomata, Takeshi. 2001. "The Power and Ideology of Artistic Creation: Elite Craft Specialists in Classic Maya Society." *Current Anthropology* 42 (3): 321–49. https://doi.org/10.1086/320475.

Institute of Archaeology, Chinese Academy of Social Sciences. 1980. *Yinxu Fu Hao Mu*. Beijing: Wenwu chubanshe.

Jaang, Li. 2023. "Erlitou: The Making of a Secondary State and a New Sociopolitical Order in Early Bronze Age China." *Journal of Archaeological Research* 31 (2): 209–62. https://doi.org/10.1007/s10814-022-09173-9.

Jiang, Yude. 2012. "Guo Zhi Dashi: Shangdai Wanqizhong de Lizhi Gailiang." In *Yinxu Yu Shang Wenhua: Yinxu Kexue Fajue 80 Nian Xueshu Jinianhui*, edited by Jigen Tang, and Zhanyue Yue, 267–76. Beijing: Science Press.

Jing, Zhichun, Tang Jigen, George Rapp, and James Stoltman. 2013. "Recent Discoveries and Some Thoughts on Early Urbanization at Anyang." In *A Companion to Chinese Archaeology*, edited by Anne P. Underhill, 343–66. Hoboken: Wiley. https://doi.org/10.1002/9781118325698.ch17.

Keightley, David. 2012. *Working for His Majesty: Research Notes on Labor Mobilization in Late Shang China (ca. 1200–1045 B.C.), as Seen in the Oracle-Bone Inscriptions, with Particular Attention to Handicraft Industries, Agriculture, Warfare, Hunting, Construction, and the Shang's Legacies*. Berkeley: Institute of East Asian Studies, University of California.

Keightley, David N. 1983. "The Late Shang State: When, Where, and What?" In *The Origins of Chinese Civilization*, edited by David N. Keightley, 523–64. Berkeley: University of California Press. https://doi.org/10.1525/9780520310797-021.

⸻ 1985. *Sources of Shang History: The Oracle-Bone Inscriptions of Bronze Age China*. Berkeley: University of California Press.

⸻ 2000. *The Ancestral Landscape: Time, Space, and Community in Late Shang China, ca. 1200–1045 B.C.* Berkeley: University of California.

2004. "The Making of the Ancestors: Late Shang Religion and Its Legacy." In *Lagerwey, Religion and Chinese Society: A Centennial Conference of the École Française d'Extrême-Orient / Vol. 1 Ancient and Medieval China*, edited by John Lagerwey, 3–63. Hong Kong: Chinese University Press.

Kirch, Patrick Vinton. 2012. *A Shark Going Inland Is My Chief: The Island Civilization of Ancient Hawai'i*. Berkeley: University of California Press.

Lam, Wengcheong. 2014. "Everything Old Is New Again?: Rethinking the Transition to Cast Iron Production in the Central Plains of China." *Journal of Anthropological Research* 70 (4): 511–42. https://doi.org/10.3998/jar.0521004.0070.402.

Lee, Gyoung-Ah, Gary W. Crawford, Li Liu, and Xingcan Chen. 2007. "Plants and People from the Early Neolithic to Shang Periods in North China." *Proceedings of the National Academy of Sciences* 104 (3): 1087–92. https://doi.org/10.1073/pnas.0609763104.

Li, Feng. 2008. *Bureaucracy and the State in Early China: Governing the Western Zhou*. Cambridge: Cambridge University Press.

Li, Ji. 1977. *Anyang*. Seattle: University of Washington Press.

Li, Suting, Roderick Campbell, and Yanfeng Hou. 2018. "Guandimiao: A Shang Village Site and Its Significance." *Antiquity* 92 (366): 1511–29. https://doi.org/10.15184/aqy.2018.176.

Li, Yung-ti. 2003. "On the Function of Cowries in Shang and Western Zhou China." *Journal of East Asian Archaeology* 5 (1): 1–26. https://doi.org/10.1163/156852303776172999.

2019. *Kingly Crafts: The Archaeology of Craft Production in Late Shang China*. New York: Columbia University Press.

Li, Zhipeng. 2009. "Yinxu dongwu yicun yanjiu." PhD, Beijing: Zhongguo Shehuikexueyuan, Kaogu Yanjiusuo.

Li, Zhipeng, and Roderick Campbell. 2019. "Puppies for the Ancestors: The Many Roles of Shang Dogs." *Archaeological Research in Asia* 17 (March): 161–72. https://doi.org/10.1016/j.ara.2018.12.001.

Li, Zhipeng, Roderick Campbell, Katherine Brunson, Jie Yang, and Yang Tao. 2014. "The Exploitation of Domestic Animal Products from the Late Neolithic Age to the Early Bronze Age in the Heartland of Ancient China." In *Animal Secondary Products: Animal Secondary Products*, edited by Haskel J. Greenfield. Oxford: Oxbow Books. https://doi.org/10.2307/j.ctvh1dr4j.

Li, Zhipeng, Yuling He, and Yude Jiang. 2011. "Yinxu Wanqi Zhigu Zuofang Yu Zhigu Shougongye de Yanjiu Huigu Tantao." *Sandai Kaogu* 4: 1–10.

Lin, Yun. 2019. "Jiaguwen zhong de Shangdai Fangguo Lianmeng." In *Gu shi juan*, edited by Lin Yun, 33–55. Lin Yun wen ji / Lin Yun zhu 2. Shang hai: Shanghai guji chubanshe.

Liu, Li. 2006. "Urbanization in China: Erlitou and Its Hinterland." In *Urbanism in the Preindustrial World: Cross-Cultural Approaches*, edited by Storey Glenn, 161–89. Tuscaloosa: University of Alabama Press. https://api.semanticscholar.org/CorpusID:130343253.

Liu, Li, and Hong Xu. 2007. "Rethinking Erlitou: Legend, History and Chinese Archaeology." *Antiquity* 81 (314): 886–901. https://doi.org/10.1017/S0003598X00095983.

Liu, Li, and Xingcan Chen. 2003. *State Formation in Early China*. Duckworth Debates on Archaeology. London: Duckworth.

— eds. 2012a. "Chinese Archaeology: Past, Present, and Future." In *The Archaeology of China: From the Late Paleolithic to the Early Bronze Age*, 1–21. Cambridge World Archaeology. Cambridge: Cambridge University Press. https://doi.org/10.1017/CBO9781139015301.002.

— 2012b. *The Archaeology of China: From the Late Paleolithic to the Early Bronze Age*, 1st ed. Cambridge: Cambridge University Press. https://doi.org/10.1017/CBO9781139015301.

Liu, Li, Xingcan Chen, and Baoping Li. 2007. "Non-state Crafts in the Early Chinese State: An Archaeological View from the Erlitou Hinterland." *Bulletin of the Indo-Pacific Prehistory Association* 27: 93–102. https://doi.org/10.7152/bippa.v27i0.11980.

Liu, Ruiliang, Mark Pollard, Jessica Rawson, et al. 2019. "Panlongcheng, Zhengzhou and the Movement of Metal in Early Bronze Age China." *Journal of World Prehistory* 32 (4): 393–428. https://doi.org/10.1007/s10963-019-09137-w.

Ma, Chengyuan. 1986. *Shang Zhou qingtongqi mingwen xuan*. Beijing: Wenwu chubanshe.

Ma, Xiaolin, Xingtao Wei, and Yanfeng Hou. 2015. "Sanmenxia Lijiayao Yizhi Chutu Guliao Yanjiu." *Wenwu* 2015 (6): 39–48.

Meng, Xianwu, and Guichang Li. 2004. "Yinxu Siheyuan Shi Jianzhu Jizhi Kaocha." *Zhongyuan Wenwu* 2004 (5): 26–31.

Puett, Michael J. 2004. *To Become a God: Cosmology, Sacrifice, and Self-Divinization in Early China*, 1 paperback ed. Harvard-Yenching Institute Monographs Series 57. Cambridge, Massachusetts: Harvard University Press.

Qian, Wei, and Xing Huang. 2021. "Invention of Cast Iron Smelting in Early China: Archaeological Survey and Numerical Simulation." *Advances in Archaeomaterials* 2 (1): 4–14. https://doi.org/10.1016/j.aia.2021.04.001.

Qiu, Xigui. 1993. "Shuo Yinxu Buci de 'dian' – Shilun Shang Ren Chuzhi Fushuzhe de Yi Zhong Fangfa." *Bulletin of the Institute of History and Philology, Academia Sinica* 64 (3): 659–86.
Schwartz, Adam. 2013. "Huayuanzhuang East I: A Study and Annotated Translation of the Oracle Bone Inscriptions." PhD dissertation, Chicago, Illinois: The University of Chicago.
Shelach, Gideon. 1996. "The Qiang and the Question of Human Sacrifice in the Late Shang Period." *Asian Perspectives* 35 (1): 1–16.
Shelach, Gideon, and Yitzhak Jaffe. 2014. "The Earliest States in China: A Long-Term Trajectory Approach." *Journal of Archaeological Research* 22 (4): 327–64. https://doi.org/10.1007/s10814-014-9074-8.
Shelach-Lavi, Gideon. 2015. *The Archaeology of Early China: From Prehistory to the Han Dynasty*. New York: Cambridge University Press.
Stoltman, James, Zhichun Jing, Jigen Tang, and George Rapp. 2009. "Ceramic Production in Shang Societies of Anyang." *Asian Perspectives* 48 (1): 182–203.
Sun, Zhouyong. 2008. *Craft Production in the Western Zhou Dynasty (1046–771 BC): A Case Study of a Jue-Earrings Workshop at the Predynastic Capital Site, Zhouyuan, China*. BAR International Series 1777. Oxford: Archaeopress.
Tang, Jigen. 2004. "The Social Organization of Late Shang China: A Mortuary Perspective." London: University College London.
2009. *Yinxu: yige wangchao de beijing*. Beijing: Kexue chubanshe.
Thote, Alain. 2014. "Zhou Bronze Workshops and the Creative Work of Design and Decoration." *Rao Zongyi Guoxueyuan Yuankan* 2014 (1): 27–54.
Underhill, Anne P., and Hui Fang. 2004. "Early State Economic Systems in China." In *Archaeological Perspectives on Political Economies*, edited by Gary M. Feinman, and Linda M. Nicholas, 129–44. Salt Lake City: University of Utah Press.
Vainker, Shelagh, ed. 2004. *Chinese Silk: A Cultural History*. New Brunswick, New Jersey: Rutgers University Press.
Von Glahn, Richard. 2016. *The Economic History of China: From Antiquity to the Nineteenth Century*, 1st ed. Cambridge: Cambridge University Press. https://doi.org/10.1017/CBO9781139343848.
Wang, Hua, Roderick Campbell, Hui Fang, Yanfeng Hou, and Zhipeng Li. 2022. "Small-Scale Bone Working in a Complex Economy: The Daxinzhuang Worked Bone Assemblage." *Journal of Anthropological Archaeology* 66: 1–19.
Wells, Christian, ed. 2008. *Dimensions of Ritual Economy*, 1st ed. Research in Economic Anthropology 27. Bingley: Emerald.

Wolin, Daniela. 2018. "Everyday Stress, Exceptional Suffering: Bioarchaeology of Violence and Personhood in Late Shang, China." PhD dissertation. New Haven : Yale University.

Yang, Bin. 2011. "The Rise and Fall of Cowrie Shells: The Asian Story." *Journal of World History* 22 (1): 1–25.

Yang, Shengnan, and Jifan Ma. 2010. *Shangdai Jingji Yu Keji*, Vol. 6. Shang Dai Shi. Beijing: Zhongguo shehuikexue chubanshe.

Yates, Robin D. S. 2001. "Slavery in Early China: A Socio-Cultural Approach." *Journal of East Asian Archaeology* 3: 283–331.

Ye, Wansong and Fuwei Yu. 1985. "Luoyang Beiyao Xizhou Yizhi Taoqi de Fenxi Yanjiu." *Kaogu* 1985 (9): 834–42.

Yinxu Work Team. 2004. "Survey and Test Excavation of the Huanbei Shang City in Anyang." Trans. Zhicun Jin. In *Chinese Archaeology* 4: 1–20.

Yinxu Xiaomintun Archaeological Team. 2008. "The Shang Building Remains at Xiaomintun in Anyang City." *Chinese Archaeology* 8 (1): 8–15. https://doi.org/10.1515/CHAR.2008.8.1.8.

Yuan, Jing, and Rod Campbell. 2009. "Recent Archaeometric Research on 'the Origins of Chinese Civilisation'." *Antiquity* 83 (319): 96–109. https://doi.org/10.1017/S0003598X00098112.

Yuan, Jing, Roderick Campbell, Lorenzo Castellano, and Chen Xianglong. 2020. "Subsistence and Persistence: Agriculture in the Central Plains of China through the Neolithic to Bronze Age Transition." *Antiquity* 94 (376): 900–915. https://doi.org/10.15184/aqy.2020.80.

Yuan, Jing, and Rowan Flad. 2005. "New Zooarchaeological Evidence for Changes in Shang Dynasty Animal Sacrifice." *Journal of Anthropological Archaeology* 24 (3): 252–70. https://doi.org/10.1016/j.jaa.2005.03.001.

Zhang, Changping. 2014. "Erligang: A Perspective from Panlongcheng." In *Art and Archaeology of the Erligang Civilization*, edited by Kyle Steinke. Princeton, New Jersey: P.Y. and Kinmay W. Tang Center for East Asian Art, Department of Art and Archaeology, Princeton University in association with Princeton University Press, pp. 51–63.

Zhang, Chi, Mark Pollard, Jessica Rawson, et al. 2019. "China's Major Late Neolithic Centres and the Rise of Erlitou." *Antiquity* 93 (369): 588–603. https://doi.org/10.15184/aqy.2019.63.

Zhang, Yan. 2022. "Feeding Status: A Comparative Study of Animal Foodways and Social Status in the Chinese Bronze Age (Guandimiao, Anyang, and Zhougongmiao, 13th–18th Century BCE)." PhD dissertation, New York: New York University.

Zhao, Hao. 2017. "Mass Bone-Working Industry in the Western Zhou Period (1046–771 BC)." PhD dissertation, Stanford: Stanford University.

Zhengzhou daxue lishixueyuan. 2014. *Dengfeng Nanwa: 2004–2006 Tianye Kaogu Baogao*. Beijing: Kexue chubanshe.

Zhongguo she hui ke xue yuan, ed. 2003. *Zhongguo Kao Gu Xue: Xia Shang Juan*. Beijing: Zhongguo shehuikexue chubanshe.

ed. 2014. *Erlitou (1999–2006)*. Beijing: Wenwu chubanshe.

Zhongguo shehuikexueyuan kaogu yanjiusuo. 1980. Yinxu Fu Hao Mu (The Tomb of Fu Hao). Beijing: Wenwu chubanshe.

2012. "Henan Anyangshi Liujiazhuang Beidi Zhitao Zuofang Yizhi de Fajue." *Kaogu* 2012(12): 43–58.

2013. *Yan shi shang cheng*. 偃师商城: 第一卷, v. 1. Beijing: Kexue chubanshe. https://books.google.com/books?id=74NLAQAACAAJ.

2014. *Anyang Dasikong: 2004 Nian Fajue Baogao*. Beijing: Wenwu chubanshe. https://books.google.com/books?id=9nSmoAEACAAJ.

Zhouyuan kaogudui. 2011. "Zhouyuan Zhuangli Xizhou Zhutong Yizhi 2003 Yu 2004 Nian Chunji Fajue Bao." *Kaoguxuebao* 2011(2): 245–316.

Zhu, Fenghan. 1990. *Shang Zhou Jia Zu Xing Tai Yan Jiu*. Tianjin: Tianjin guji chubanshe.

Cambridge Elements

Ancient and Pre-modern Economies

Kenneth G. Hirth
The Pennsylvania State University

Ken Hirth's research focuses on the development of ranked and state-level societies in the New World. He is interested in political economy and how forms of resource control lead to the development of structural inequalities. Topics of special interest include: exchange systems, craft production, settlement patterns, and preindustrial urbanism. Methodological interests include: lithic technology and use-wear, ceramics, and spatial analysis.

Timothy Earle
Northwestern University

Timothy Earle is an economic anthropologist specializing in the archaeological studies of social inequality, leadership, and political economy in early chiefdoms and states. He has conducted field projects in Polynesia, Peru, Argentina, Denmark, and Hungary. Having studied the emergence of social complexity in three world regions, his work is comparative, searching for the causes of alternative pathways to centralized power.

Emily J. Kate
University of Vienna

Emily Kate is bioarchaeologist with training in radiocarbon dating, isotopic studies, human osteology, and paleodemography. Having worked with projects from Latin America and Europe, her interests include the manner in which paleodietary trends can be used to assess shifts in social and political structure, the affect of migration on societies, and the refinement of regional chronologies through radiocarbon programs.

About the Series

Elements in Ancient and Pre-modern Economies is committed to critical scholarship on the comparative economies of traditional societies. Volumes either focus on case studies of well documented societies, providing information on domestic and institutional economies, or provide comparative analyses of topical issues related to economic function. Each Element adopts an innovative and interdisciplinary view of culture and economy, offering authoritative discussions of how societies survived and thrived throughout human history.

Cambridge Elements

Ancient and Pre-modern Economies

Elements in the Series

Ancient and Pre-modern Economies of the North American Pacific Northwest
Anna Marie Prentiss

The Aztec Economy
Frances F. Berdan

Shell Money: A Comparative Study
Mikael Fauvelle

A Historical Ethnography of the Enga Economy of Papua New Guinea
Polly Wiessner, Akii Tumu and Nitze Pupu

Ancient Maya Economies
Scott R. Hutson

Nordic Bronze Age Economies
Christian Horn, Knut Ivar Austvoll, Magnus Artursson and Johan Ling

Economies of the Inca World
R. Alan Covey and Jordan Dalton

The Shang Economy
Roderick Campbell

A full series listing is available at: www.cambridge.org/EAPE

For EU product safety concerns, contact us at Calle de José Abascal, 56–1°, 28003 Madrid, Spain or eugpsr@cambridge.org.

www.ingramcontent.com/pod-product-compliance
Lightning Source LLC
LaVergne TN
LVHW020351260326
834688LV00045B/1666